TO:

....

FROM:

....

DATE:

....

Just Breathe

DEVOTIONS &
PRAYERS
for the
OVERWHELMED
HEART

BARBOUR
PUBLISHING

Devotions by Terry Alburger, Emily Biggers, Jean Fischer, Renae Green, Shanna D. Gregor, Linda Hang, Anita Higman, Eileen Key, Ardythe Kolb, Shelley R. Lee, Marian Leslie, Donna K. Maltese, Kelly McIntosh, Hillary McMullen, Lydia Mindling, MariLee Parrish, Valorie Quesenberry, Shana Schutte, Carey Scott, Karin Dahl Silver, Rae Simons, Janice Thompson, Stacey Thureen, Annie Tipton, and Amy Trent.

Scripture quotations marked KJV are taken from the King James Version of the Bible.

Scripture quotations marked NIV are taken from the HOLY BIBLE, NEW INTERNATIONAL VERSION®. NIV®. Copyright © 1973, 1978, 1984, 2011 by Biblica, Inc.™ Used by permission. All rights reserved worldwide.

Scripture quotations marked NLT are taken from the *Holy Bible*. New Living Translation copyright© 1996, 2004, 2015 by Tyndale House Foundation. Used by permission of Tyndale House Publishers, Inc. Carol Stream, Illinois 60188. All rights reserved.

Scripture quotations marked NASB are taken from the New American Standard Bible, © 1960, 1962, 1963, 1968, 1971, 1972, 1973, 1975, 1977, 1995, 2020 by The Lockman Foundation. Used by permission.

Scripture quotations marked AMPC are taken from the Amplified® Bible, Classic Edition, Copyright © 1954, 1958, 1962, 1964, 1965, 1987 by The Lockman Foundation. Used by permission.

Scripture quotations marked NCV are taken from the New Century Version of the Bible, copyright © 2005 by Thomas Nelson, Inc. Used by permission. All rights reserved.

Scripture quotations marked MSG are from *THE MESSAGE*. Copyright © by Eugene H. Peterson 1993, 1994, 1995, 1996, 2000, 2001, 2002. Used by permission of NavPress Publishing Group.

Scripture quotations marked NKJV are taken from the New King James Version®. Copyright © 1982 by Thomas Nelson, Inc. Used by permission. All rights reserved.

Scripture quotations marked HCSB are taken from the Holman Christian Standard Bible ® Copyright © 1999, 2000, 2002, 2003, 2009 by Holman Bible Publishers. Used by permission.

Scripture quotations marked ESV are from The Holy Bible, English Standard Version®, copyright © 2001 by Crossway Bibles, a publishing ministry of Good News Publishers. The ESV® text has been reproduced in cooperation with and by permission of Good News Publishers. Unauthorized reproduction of this publication is prohibited. All rights reserved.

Published by Barbour Publishing, Inc., 1810 Barbour Drive, Uhrichsville, Ohio 44683, www.barbourbooks.com

Our mission is to inspire the world with the life-changing message of the Bible.

Member of the
Evangelical Christian
Publishers Association

Printed in China.

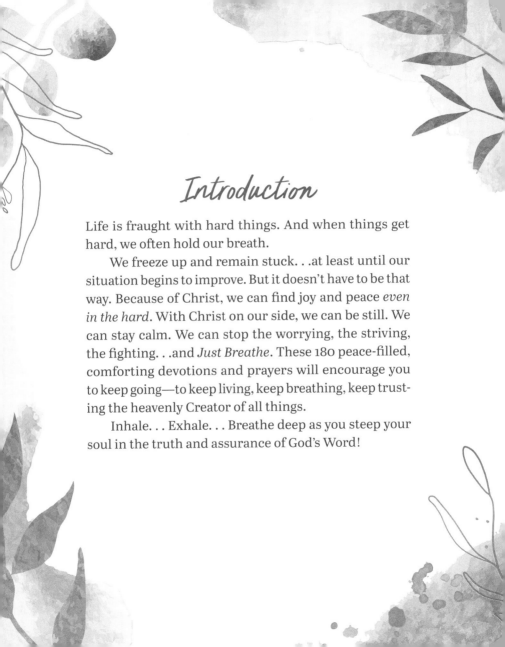

Introduction

Life is fraught with hard things. And when things get hard, we often hold our breath.

We freeze up and remain stuck. . .at least until our situation begins to improve. But it doesn't have to be that way. Because of Christ, we can find joy and peace *even in the hard*. With Christ on our side, we can be still. We can stay calm. We can stop the worrying, the striving, the fighting. . .and *Just Breathe*. These 180 peace-filled, comforting devotions and prayers will encourage you to keep going—to keep living, keep breathing, keep trusting the heavenly Creator of all things.

Inhale. . . Exhale. . . Breathe deep as you steep your soul in the truth and assurance of God's Word!

His Delight

"The LORD your God is with you, the Mighty Warrior who saves. He will take great delight in you; in his love he will no longer rebuke you, but will rejoice over you with singing."
ZEPHANIAH 3:17 NIV

Delight. What a wonderful word! The connotations are enjoyment and pleasure, joy and gladness. You are usually delighted when something has pleased you. Maybe it's the song of a bird, the chatter of your child, or simply a quiet, starry night that soothes your senses and fills your heart with satisfaction.

Scripture tells us the Lord will take delight in us and will rejoice over us with singing. Imagine that! The very Mighty Warrior of the universe relishing His creation. And that creation is you. It's hard to imagine when we have dirty faces or are out of sorts that He could care for us at all. But it's true. Our God saves and loves. Our God is truth and mercy. He loves His children.

Take a deep breath and carve out some time to appreciate and bask in the truth of the Bible. God loves *you* and He delights in *you*. You are the apple of His eye. Reach out a hand to Him this day, knowing full well He will interlace His fingers with yours and never let go. Selah. Pause and reflect.

Father God, how we love You. We do not understand the depth and breadth of Your love for us, but we are ever so grateful. Amen.

Sabbath Rest

Now, since God has left us the promise that we may enter his rest, let us be very careful so none of you will fail to enter.
HEBREWS 4:1 NCV

We move at such a rapid pace. Life tugs and pulls at us, and we respond, sprinting toward goal after goal. What overachievers we are!

The Lord never intended for us to go around the clock. He didn't design our bodies to run in "energizer bunny" mode 24-7. We can live like this for a little while, sure. But eventually, something's got to give, and it's usually our health. Or our emotions. Or our relationships. Or—worst of all—our times of intimacy with God.

We are created in the image of God, and He is always on the move! Still, He instituted the Sabbath because He knows mankind's tendency to go, go, go. Sure, we have work to do. Yes, we have people to care for and souls to reach. But if we're broken down from lack of sleep or from overextending ourselves, there won't be anything to offer others. So, slow down! Take a breather. For that matter, take a nap. And don't apologize for it! Moments of respite are precious.

Lord, thank You for the reminder that You want me to rest. It's not always easy. I'm such a go-getter, but I have to confess that taking a break feels really, really good. Draw me away to Your side for a special time of rest, I pray.

Standing Still

You shall not need to fight in this battle; take your positions,
stand still, and see the deliverance of the Lord [Who
is] with you. . . . Fear not nor be dismayed. Tomorrow
go out against them, for the Lord is with you.
2 CHRONICLES 20:17 AMPC

King Jehoshaphat made all the right moves when it came to a major army rising up against him and his people. His first step was to humbly seek God's face. His second, to keep his eyes on his Lord. Because Jehoshaphat took these bold steps, God gave him a good word. The king and his people need not fight this great army but merely hold their positions and watch what God was going to do! They were neither to fear nor freak out, because when they headed out to meet the enemy, the All-Powerful would be with them!

When God's daughters—princesses in their own right—seek their Father's face, focus on Him alone, then take a firm stance with courage and conviction, knowing that God will fight whatever challenge approaches, nothing can defeat them! Holding this knowledge close to her heart, a woman remains calm, empowered, and faithful—able to lead herself and others. This "standing still" is evidence of God's unique and awesome power in this frenzied, fast-paced society. How delightful to be a woman firmly planted in faith, filled with the serenity of her Savior.

Help me to stand still, Lord. Give me the confidence to
know You are with me every step of the way. Calm the
fast beating of my heart as I lean back upon You.

Creator God

"You are worthy, O Lord our God, to receive glory and honor and power. For you created all things, and they exist because you created what you pleased."
REVELATION 4:11 NLT

What's your favorite part of God's creation?

A fiery summer sunset?

A sparkling blue-green ocean?

A glistening snowflake?

A multicolored carpet of wildflowers?

Whatever you delight in, know that the Creator God is worthy of your praise for His incomparable artistry and creativity. Without Him, *nothing* would exist. In fact, everything is dependent on Him—including you and me! And the God who created all things also sustains all things.

Can you think of anything better? What worries and concerns do you need to carry if God is in control? If all of creation is entirely up to Him, what do you need to stress and fret about?

Not one single thing! You don't need to have a care in the world when you have complete faith and understanding that God's got it all—the entire world and everything in it—in His very capable hands.

So, let go of your worries today and give the Lord glory and honor for His beautiful and wonderful creation.

Creator God, although I sometimes take Your creation for granted, I know You are worthy of my daily praise— every time I enjoy the beauty of a sunset or take pleasure in the colorful landscape of autumn. I want to have a grateful heart always. Thank You, Father.

More Jesus

*"Are you tired? Worn out? Burned out on religion?
Come to me. Get away with me and you'll recover your life.
I'll show you how to take a real rest. Walk with me and work
with me—watch how I do it. Learn the unforced rhythms of
grace. I won't lay anything heavy or ill-fitting on you. Keep
company with me and you'll learn to live freely and lightly."*
MATTHEW 11:28–30 MSG

When was the last time you had a real, honest-to-goodness rest?. . . The kind that refreshes you both mentally and physically. . . Rest that makes you feel completely revitalized and alive!

If that sounds like wishful thinking—if your mind tells you, *Yeah, right! I haven't had a good rest in at least ten years—and there's no end in sight for me!*—take these words from Matthew 11 to heart. Jesus says, "Get away with me. . . . I'll show you how to take a real rest." What a promise!

Instead of more *busy* in your life, get more of *Jesus*. He is just what your weary soul needs. He will pull you from the depths of your day-to-day burnout and give you rest like you're never experienced it before—a rest that leads to free and light living! Praise Him!

*Father God, Rest-Giver, comfort my world-weary
soul today. I am exhausted! I trust You to show
me the way to refreshing rest. Thank You!*

Reap Righteousness

But the wisdom that comes from heaven is first of all pure;
then peace-loving, considerate, submissive, full of mercy and
good fruit, impartial and sincere. Peacemakers who
sow in peace reap a harvest of righteousness.
JAMES 3:17–18 NIV

James wrote about two types of wisdom. There's the world's wisdom, which is characterized by "bitter envy and selfish ambition" (James 3:14 NIV). And then there's the wisdom that we believers find as we trust in God. This wisdom produces great characteristics within us, such as peace, humility, mercy, and more. The qualities take time to reap, but, as you continue trusting God, they will become a more natural part of who you are.

But how do you get there from here? By listening to God. Solomon himself wrote in Proverbs 21:11 (MSG), "Simpletons only learn the hard way, but the wise learn by listening."

Are you listening to God? Take a little inventory: How is the noise level in your life? Are you constantly running from one thing to the next? Do you feel worn out? Are you constantly filling what could be quiet time with constant chatter or noise like the radio, TV, or other forms of media?

If you want to reap the wisdom and righteousness that come from trusting in God, then take some quiet time to be still and listen.

Lord, in these moments I have with You right now, help me
listen to Your promptings. Help me to trust You more.

Hanging On

*He spreads out the northern skies over empty
space; he suspends the earth over nothing.*
JOB 26:7 NIV

An old, dry petunia bloom had fallen from its hanging pot and was caught in a mere two-threaded spiderweb. Suspended in midair, it was seemingly held by nothing at all and flittered wildly in the softest of breezes. God and the curious cat are likely the only ones who knew how long it had been there.

Do you ever feel this way? Barely hanging on, struggling like crazy, and no one seems to notice. When the struggle *is* recognized by others, they can't see why it's so hard; and then, on top of your hardship, you may be judged too. Sometimes the only person who notices knocks you around, like the cat leaping and batting at the hovering debris.

Does God notice? Is He going to help you?

Remember that God absolutely notices and cares immensely. He holds up the universe, and He holds you up even when you feel alone, mocked, and discouraged. He will not forget your plight.

*Lord God, thank You for knowing exactly where we
are all the time and for holding us up even when we
don't understand the hows and the whys. Amen.*

Finding God in Life's Struggles

And I want you to know, my dear brothers and sisters,
that everything that has happened to me here has helped to
spread the Good News. For everyone here, including the whole
palace guard, knows that I am in chains because of Christ.

PHILIPPIANS 1:12–13 NLT

It's possible to welcome suffering into your life.

Are you kidding me? you're probably wondering. *Why would I do* that*?!*

The apostle Paul wrote his letter to the Philippians from behind the lock and key of a jail cell. It was just one of several times in his life when he was arrested or imprisoned for preaching the truth of Jesus. But his own suffering didn't come as a surprise to him. Jesus tells us in John 16, "Here on earth you will have many trials and sorrows. But take heart, because I have overcome the world" (v. 33 NLT).

So, when difficult times come, find strength in the fact that no situation comes as a surprise to God. Look for His guiding hand. Ask for His intervention. Don't be afraid of tomorrow. Pray for His peace. Tap into real, lasting joy that's based on the goodness of God rather than on your circumstances. Find contentment in His love, a powerful force that remains no matter how difficult life gets. Finally, lean on Jesus, the Savior who has already conquered the darkness of the world for all time.

Jesus, I will welcome trials and sorrows when they
come. You have already overcome them! Amen.

Confident Peace

*I have told you these things, so that in Me you may
have [perfect] peace and confidence. In the world you
have tribulation and trials and distress and frustration;
but be of good cheer [take courage; be confident, certain,
undaunted]! For I have overcome the world. [I have deprived
it of power to harm you and have conquered it for you.]*
JOHN 16:33 AMPC

The apostle Paul called the peace Jesus spoke of in this passage *incomprehensible*, not easy to comprehend or understand with our finite minds (Philippians 4:7). Part of the armor of God that Paul later describes in Ephesians 6 is the footwear, the sandals—the gospel of peace. God has much to say about peace in the Bible. A quiet spirit, a peaceful spirit, is what God desires for each of His children. Yet, worry in the midst of our busyness is much more common.

The scriptures tell us all we need to know in order to live a life of peace, of contentment, free from the worry and distraction of the world. Replacing the worry-thoughts with things that are true, honorable, right, pure, lovely, admirable, excellent, and worthy of praise (Philippians 4:8) will make room for the peace from God that transcends human understanding. Jesus gives it freely to all who desire to follow His example. Claim it today.

*Father, as I take every thought captive to the glory of Jesus
Christ, help me to think on the things Paul listed in Philippians.
May Your peace reign in my heart and life today.*

Lord, Help!

"LORD, help!" they cried in their trouble, and he saved them from their distress. He calmed the storm to a whisper and stilled the waves. What a blessing was that stillness as he brought them safely into harbor!
PSALM 107:28–30 NLT

Prayers do not have to be eloquent or majestic. There are no requirements for them to be long and labored. The only thing necessary is that you communicate with God. Your words can be heart-wrenching—rising deep from the very bottom of your soul—or calm and gentle as a whisper. However you speak to Him, you can know that He hears you and will answer.

Samuel Morse, the father of modern communication, said, "The only gleam of hope, and I cannot underrate it, is from confidence in God. When I look upward it calms any apprehension for the future, and I seem to hear a voice saying: 'If I clothe the lilies of the field, shall I not also clothe you?' Here is my strong confidence, and I will wait patiently for the direction of Providence."

The answer to your prayer does not depend on you. Your expressions of your heart spoken to your Father bring Him onto the scene for any reason you need Him.

Father, thank You for hearing my prayers. I know that You are always near to me and You answer my heart's cry. Help me to come to You first instead of trying to do things on my own. Amen.

I Surrender

I will rejoice in the LORD! I will be joyful in the God of my
salvation! The Sovereign LORD is my strength! He makes me
as surefooted as a deer, able to tread upon the heights.
HABAKKUK 3:18–19 NLT

Sometimes life seems like an uphill battle, and we certainly don't feel like celebrating. We find ourselves frustrated by the demands of the day and worried about the future. It's just too difficult to stay the course—keep on keeping on. We're tempted to throw up our hands in frustration and quit. That's when we must realize we're in the perfect position: hands raised in surrender.

Learn that God's promises are true. When we relax in His care and focus on Him, He will be with us in all our difficulties. He didn't promise a life with no problems. He did promise to carry us through. In Proverbs 3:5 in the Amplified Bible, the word *trust* is extrapolated: lean on, trust in, and be confident in the Lord. Are we leaning on the Lord? Do we trust Him with our future and the future of those in our care? Have we become confident in His Word?

Surrender and *trust*. Two words which lead to life and joy. Choose to surrender and trust this day. He'll then bring you safely over the mountains.

Dear Lord, surrendering and trusting don't come naturally.
Gently guide Me so I might learn of You and become confident
in Your care. Enable me to live life to the fullest. Amen.

The Highest Calling

Let us not become weary in doing good, for at the proper
time we will reap a harvest if we do not give up.

GALATIANS 6:9 NIV

A lot of good is done in December. We shop for gifts. We cook big, delicious meals for our families. We give to charities and go out of our way to show compassion and kindness to those around us. And by the time the holiday season ends, we are bone-weary.

But sharing love, kindness, and compassion shouldn't be a seasonal habit. Of all our reasons for inhabiting space on this planet, our highest calling—our most noble purpose—is this: we were placed here to show love to other people.

Weariness never stems from living out our purpose. Rather, it seeps in when we get distracted from our purpose and pour our energy into things that don't elevate that calling. When we stay committed to our most virtuous reason for existence, we are energized.

That's not to say we won't need to rest. It takes a lot of energy to pour ourselves out for other people. But when we understand our purpose of love and we cater our actions to that purpose, the weariness is the good, hard-night's-sleep kind of weary. The stress, the anxiety, the depression that come when we don't live our purpose seem to dissipate when we continue doing good and living out our highest moral function: to love.

Dear Father, help me to live out my purpose today and
every day. Teach me to love the way You love. Amen.

Signs of His Presence

*Keep your eyes open for G<small>OD</small>, watch for his works; be alert
for signs of his presence. Remember the world of wonders
he has made, his miracles, and the verdicts he's rendered—
O seed of Abraham, his servant, O child of Jacob, his chosen.*
P<small>SALM</small> 105:5–6 <small>MSG</small>

Life is busy—on purpose! The enemy of your soul wants to keep you preoccupied, filled with any distraction that would keep your eyes off the great works God is doing.

Yet, God would have you do otherwise.

Put down your busy schedule and take a deep breath! What's God doing in your life? Perhaps, at first glance, you saw His fingerprints on your life as coincidence. Look a little closer. Where has He blessed you lately? When has He poured out His favor on you and given you opportunities you otherwise might not have had?

Where's He at work in the lives of your loved ones? How has He intervened? Has someone escaped a car wreck untouched or not been in the place they planned and so escaped tragedy?

What great work is God doing now, and how can you join Him? When you see Him at work and join Him there, your soul is awake to His presence and in tune with Him.

*God, open my eyes to see Your works. Help me
be watchful and recognize Your presence.*

The Voice

[The Lord] will still be with you to teach you. You will see your teacher with your own eyes. Your own ears will hear him. Right behind you a voice will say, "This is the way you should go," whether to the right or to the left.
ISAIAH 30:20–21 NLT

It's a fact that women hear better than men! But to whom are the ladies listening?

God wants to be the supreme voice in the life of each of His daughters. For when she follows His direction, she will not be misled. She will not be deviating from His path.

Yet, today's world holds so many competing voices, people shouting for attention. So, how does a woman of the Way know which voice is God's? By staying deep in His Word. By not just reading that Word but obeying it. By using that Word to filter all her circumstances to determine the real truth. By using that Word as a litmus test to prove all other theories, opinions, and observations.

Then, and only then, in the quiet, secret place, alone with her Savior, can she sense God's familiar presence, discern His voice, seek His direction, and determine her next step, confident that the Teacher is with her and giving her the best guidance she could ever ask for or imagine, saying, "This is the way you should go."

May You continue to speak words into my life, Lord. I thank You so much for where You've brought me thus far. And I am excited about the roads to come.

Songs of Praise

*"Great and marvelous are your works, O Lord God,
the Almighty. Just and true are your ways, O King of the
nations. Who will not fear you, Lord, and glorify your name?
For you alone are holy. All nations will come and worship
before you, for your righteous deeds have been revealed."*

REVELATION 15:3–4 NLT

Where is your focus? Are you distracted daily by your own thoughts—does your brain swirl with uncontrolled worries, cares, and stresses? Is your glass half-empty today, friend? If so, give your spirit a much-needed holy pause.

Refocus your thoughts on your heavenly Father—the one who makes all things possible (Matthew 19:26). When you turn your thoughts on Him—and not yourself—you'll be amazed at the transformation of your mindset. Just try it. . .and see what happens.

Repeat today's song of thanksgiving and praise from the book of Revelation.

The words of wonder and admiration will turn your heart to praise. Every sentence is an intentional focus on God—and His mighty works! This song is a joyful celebration of His infinite power and wisdom—and His righteousness!

Aren't you blessed to know the one and only Miracle-Worker, Truth-Teller, and Promise-Keeper? You are blessed indeed!

*Promise-Keeper, I am so blessed to have a growing relationship
with You. Please refocus my thoughts. I want to think less of
myself and more of You every day. I praise You! Amen.*

23

No Guilt, Just Grace

Yet the news about him spread all the more, so that crowds of
people came to hear him and to be healed of their sicknesses.
But Jesus often withdrew to lonely places and prayed.
LUKE 5:15–16 NIV

"You make time for things that are important to you." Do you immediately feel guilty when you read that adage? *I know, I know. I* should *make sure I get family time, prayer time, and gym time, but I'm beyond stressed even thinking about trying to add one more thing to my schedule!*

You're not alone. You know, Jesus probably felt pressures in His work too. As His fame spread, actual *multitudes* of people came to Him to be healed. Showing compassion, Jesus healed their diseases and preached God's good news. But we also see He "withdrew to lonely places" to pray. Jesus, fully God, was also fully human: He got hungry, tired, and probably emotionally drained from witnessing the brokenness in His creation firsthand. He met with the Father for rest and strength so that He could be prepared to help those who needed Him.

Get out from under the guilt and lean into His grace. God invites you to come to Him—no matter where you are or what you're doing in your day—to exchange your cares for His strength, peace, and joy. He will meet you where you are.

Jehovah Jireh, my provider, remind me
throughout today that I can always rest in You.

Rock of Escape

*Saul quit chasing David and returned to fight the
Philistines. Ever since that time, the place where David
was camped has been called the Rock of Escape.*

1 SAMUEL 23:28 NLT

Hearing that Saul was after him, David fled to a great rock and hid there. Just as Saul was about to capture David, Saul had to give up the chase and return to fight the Philistines. Ever since then, David called his hideout "the Rock of Escape."

Unsure of her footing, longing to find peace and rest, desperate for protection from circumstances, yearning for the silence only God can provide, woman also has an escape: God. "For who is God besides the LORD? And who is the Rock except our God?" (Psalm 18:31 NIV). In Him, as nowhere else, is she safe from pursuers, be they in the form of family or friends, strangers or enemies, thoughts or circumstances, things seen or unseen. Here in her "sanctuary [a sacred and indestructible asylum]" (Isaiah 8:14 AMPC), she can rest easy, soak up the quiet, gather her forces together, remember the power of the spiritual over the material, and revive herself.

But how does she get to her Rock of Escape? By stilling her mind and approaching God. By trusting in Him alone. By calling out, "My Lord! Save me!" By faithfully camping herself in His presence. By basking in His precious words of peace, comfort, and solace.

*I come to You, my Rock, my God, my refuge, my Lord.
It is in You alone that I may rest in peace and safety.*

I Am

*God said to Moses, "I AM WHO I AM. This is what you
are to say to the Israelites: 'I AM has sent me to you.'"*

EXODUS 3:14 NIV

The words "I AM" ring out in the present tense. These words are used some seven hundred times in the Bible to describe God and Jesus. When Moses was on the mount and asked God who He was, a voice thundered, "I AM." In the New Testament, Jesus said of Himself, "I am the bread of life; I am the light of the world; I am the Good Shepherd; I am the way; I am the resurrection." Present tense. Words of hope and life. I AM.

Who is God to you today? Is He in the present tense? Living, loving, presiding over your life? Is the Lord of Lords "I Was" or "I've Never Been" to you? Have you experienced the hope which comes from an everlasting "I AM" Father? One who walks by you daily and will never let go? "I am with you always."

We are surprised when we struggle in the world, yet hesitate to turn to our very Creator. He has the answers, and He will fill you with hope. Reach for Him today. Don't be uncertain. Know Him. For He is, after all, I AM.

*Father, we surrender our lives to You this day. We choose to
turn from our sins, reach for Your hand, and ask for Your
guidance. Thank You for Your loving kindness. Amen.*

Answer Me!

Answer me when I call to you, my righteous God.
Give me relief from my distress; have mercy
on me and hear my prayer.
PSALM 4:1 NIV

Have you ever felt like God wasn't listening? We've all felt that from time to time. David felt it when he slept in a cold, hard cave night after night while being pursued by Saul's men. He felt it when his son Absalom turned against him. Time and again in his life, David felt abandoned by God. And yet, David was called a man after God's own heart.

No matter our maturity level, there will be times when we feel abandoned by God. There will be times when our faith wavers and our fortitude wanes. That's okay. It's normal.

But David didn't give up. He kept crying out to God, kept falling to his knees in worship, kept storming God's presence with his pleas. David knew God wouldn't hide His face for long, for he knew what we might sometimes forget: God is love. He loves us without condition and without limit. And He is never far from those He loves.

No matter how distant God may seem, we need to keep talking to Him. Keep praying. Keep pouring out our hearts. We can know, as David knew, that God will answer in His time.

Dear Father, thank You for always hearing my prayers.
Help me to trust You, even when You seem distant. Amen.

New Things

"Look, I am about to do something new; even now it is coming. Do you not see it? Indeed, I will make a way in the wilderness, rivers in the desert."
ISAIAH 43:19 HCSB

Sometimes, it seems like we're standing in the middle of a thick forest. Lost. No way out. No path, no help to be found. Trees block the sunlight; we have no cell phone reception, no idea which way to go. At least, that's what it feels like, right?

But God says when we're in a wilderness with no clear path, He'll make a path. He'll clear a way for us if we'll just keep looking to Him and moving forward. If we turn around and try to live in the past, we'll lose our way. But if we follow Him, He'll show us a better way.

At times, it feels like we don't have the provisions we need. We struggle to pay bills, or we long for friendship or lost love. We feel physically, financially, or spiritually destitute. But even then, God will provide. When we find ourselves in a desert, God will bring a river! But in order to find that river, we can't return to our former way of life. We must keep moving forward, keep following Him, keep trusting His love for us. He is good, and all His plans for us are good. In faith, we can leave the past behind and step forward into a future filled with His bountiful provision.

Dear Father, I trust You with my future. I can't wait to see what You have in store. Amen.

Quiet Time

*"But when you pray, go away by yourself, shut the door
behind you, and pray to your Father in private. Then
your Father, who sees everything, will reward you."*

MATTHEW 6:6 NLT

Life is so noisy. Kids squabbling, televisions blaring, horns honking, people talking, coworkers arguing, phones ringing, computers dinging, text messages coming through. . .it can get crazy. Where can a woman go to find peace and quiet? Many have retreated to their bathrooms or even their closets for moments of alone time. Likely, you have your own special spot meant for getaways. (Of course, kiddos are probably beating on the door.)

In the middle of all the chaos, however, God longs for us to spend quiet time with Him. He doesn't care where this takes place—or even if it's completely silent in that place. All that matters is that you draw near to Him and tune in to hear His still, small voice. What's keeping you from doing that now? Take a few steps away from the noise and spend a little time with Him.

*How wonderful to draw close to You, Lord. I love our times
together. Peaceful. Quiet. Sweet. Intimate. Okay, I can still
hear the kids beating on the bathroom door, but that doesn't
bother me. I love every precious moment I get to spend with You.
I'm so grateful that You woo me into a place with You. Amen.*

His Majesty

*God's voice thunders in marvelous ways; he does
great things beyond our understanding.*
JOB 37:5 NIV

God is both great and good at the same time.

As far as being great, He is *El*, which means God in full power. He is the awesome creator of everything we see. He is in control of the rain, snow, and sun. He holds the earth together with His thoughts. He is God of unlimited might.

At the same time and to the same degree, God is *good.* He is marvelously and unsurpassably good. There is no darkness or evil in Him. He is 100 percent kind, loving, and merciful all the time.

Together, His greatness and His goodness mean that we can trust Him to work in our lives in an amazing way. We can trust that even when we struggle with hardships, He is working things out for our best. We can trust that when we experience success, it has been a good gift from His hand.

No matter what the circumstances of your life, you can lift your eyes to God whose voice thunders mightily. You can gratefully and humbly trust the way your great and good God designs your day.

*God, I am grateful for Your mighty strength and
goodness. Please do great things in my life today.*

Let Prayer Sustain You

Then the king was exceedingly glad and commanded that Daniel
should be taken up out of the den. So Daniel was taken up out
of the den, and no hurt of any kind was found on him because
he believed in (relied on, adhered to, and trusted in) his God.

DANIEL 6:23 AMPC

Daniel believed God was with him every moment of his day. He took time for conversations with Him. The spiritual disciplines Daniel practiced throughout his day drew him closer to God and allowed him to hear His instruction. When a decree went out across the land "that whoever petitions any god or man for thirty days" (Daniel 6:7 NKJV) be thrown into a lions' den, Daniel refused to stop the times of prayer that sustained him.

He was found out and thrown into a den of hungry lions. Supernaturally, God delivered Daniel by shutting the lions' mouths so that they could not harm him.

Life for most moves at a frenzied pace. Last minute interruptions and busy schedules can easily push your time with God completely out of your day. Are you disciplined in prayer? If God can shut the lions' mouths for Daniel, He can give you the time you need to do what's important when you give your time to Him in prayer first.

God, You have brought me through some pretty tough
situations. Each time my confidence in You grows.
Help me value my time with You above all else.

Movers and Shakers

"But as for you, be strong and do not give up,
for your work will be rewarded."
2 CHRONICLES 15:7 NIV

Women love to accomplish tasks. They work around the clock, taking on responsibilities that often test their strength and their health. Many times, they say yes when they should say no. (Perhaps you can relate!) Today, take some time to assess your obligations. If there's too much "moving and shaking" going on in your life, maybe it's time to trim back and use that *no* word.

Perhaps you're on the opposite end of the spectrum. You wish you could get the energy to set some goals, but you're too wiped out. Maybe it's time to check your diet and exercise plan to see if you can get some relief by eating better or getting the rest you need.

One thing's for sure: God wants His daughters to accomplish great things for Him. When you're overworked or exhausted, that won't happen. Balance, my friend! It's what holds every schedule together!

Lord, I want to be a mover and shaker for You. I don't want my days
to pass without being effective for the kingdom. Keep me motivated,
Father, and help me to do my best, but show me when I've crossed
over a line. All things in balance, Father. That's my prayer. Amen.

Fix Your Thoughts on Truth

And now, dear brothers and sisters, one final thing.
Fix your thoughts on what is true, and honorable,
and right, and pure, and lovely, and admirable. Think
about things that are excellent and worthy of praise.
PHILIPPIANS 4:8 NLT

In a world loaded with mixed messages and immorality of every kind, it becomes increasingly difficult to have pure thoughts and clear minds. What can a believer do to keep her mind set on Christ? Replace the negative message with a positive message from God's Word.

Think about the negative messages that you struggle with the most. Maybe you struggle with some of these: You're not thin enough. You're not spiritual enough. You've made a lot of mistakes, etc.

Dig through the scriptures and find truth from God's Word to combat the false message that you're struggling with. Write the passages down and memorize them. Here are a few to get you started:

- God looks at my heart, not my outward appearance. (1 Samuel 16:7)
- I am free in Christ. (1 Corinthians 1:30)
- I am a new creation. My old self is gone! (2 Corinthians 5:17)

The next time you feel negativity and false messages slip into your thinking, fix your thoughts on what you know to be true. Pray for the Lord to replace the doubts and negativity with His words of truth.

Lord God, please control my thoughts and help
me set my mind and heart on You alone. Amen.

He Can Do All

*Then Job answered the L*ORD *and said: "I know
that You can do everything, and that no purpose
of Yours can be withheld from You."*
JOB 42:1–2 NKJV

Do we live in the knowledge that the Lord can do all things? Or do we walk each day hesitantly, as though He won't provide or will not answer our call? So very often we doubt, and our faith is small. How is it that we can worship such a great, vast God and have such a tiny belief?

Our unbelief robs God of His due glory and honor and it chains us to insecurity. There is nothing more powerful than the Lord; do we live as though this is truth? We store up so much knowledge of God's Word and promises in our heads, but we never let them settle and grow in our hearts. We keep them stashed away as nice facts that we can access when sorrow sets in, like aspirin for muscle pain, but we do not live by them. We need the Lord to help us place them in our hearts, as a seal. We need Him to help us bind them around our necks so that we are ever conscious of the Lord.

*Father, there are many times that I act like and believe that
You are not in control of a situation. I run around trying to fix
things and end up making it worse. Lord, forgive me, and help
me to pause, pray, and listen for Your instruction. Amen.*

The One Choice That Brings Peace

You will keep in perfect peace those whose minds
are steadfast, because they trust in you.
ISAIAH 26:3 NIV

For the woman who wants to experience the peace God promises, there are only two choices: trust or torment. We must ask ourselves, "Will I rely on God, choosing to believe He can be trusted with all I don't understand and the concerns that consume my thoughts, or will I choose not to believe and trust Him?" The first choice brings rest and peace. The latter only brings torment.

Isaiah 30:15 (NLT) says, "In quietness and confidence is your strength." The one who chooses belief and trust experiences a confidence and quietness of spirit. The one who chooses not to believe and not to trust her Lord experiences a lack of confidence, and chaos overtakes her spirit. "What will happen now?" "Oh no! Awful things are going to happen; I just know it!" In this there is torment.

Belief and trust are chosen because life will always give you many reasons not to trust. It seems that every difficult experience invites us to unbelief, to focus on all that is going wrong and to look to the future in fear. It's not easy to make the choice to believe and trust because it's willful. It's deliberate. And sometimes it's moment by moment.

Lord, please help me to choose trust each moment today
so I can live in the abundance of Your peace. Amen.

Lead My Heart

May the Lord lead your hearts into a full understanding
and expression of the love of God and the patient
endurance that comes from Christ.

2 THESSALONIANS 3:5 NLT

We can't begin to comprehend all God does for us. Even before we allow Him to lead us, He is part of our universe. Without Him, the world would be devoid of love, kindness, joy, patience, or anything positive that people take for granted and expect. His love directs the events of the entire cosmos—heaven and earth—with or without the consent of individuals or governments.

The Lord yearns to direct each of our hearts so we understand the patient, enduring love of Christ. Why would anyone resist? It makes no sense, yet we're all guilty of going our own way sometimes, not allowing the one who created us to complete His masterpiece the way He wants.

If we try to control our own destiny, we flounder and our lives are full of confusion. We search for love in the things of this world and find broken hearts. We seek joy only to face emptiness. We convince ourselves there is no truth because we ignore reality. We waste time searching for things that bring no satisfaction.

When we bow our hearts and minds to the Creator and follow Him, we can bask in the calm of His unwavering peace. He leads us into a full understanding of true love and abundant life.

Dear Father, I ask You to continually fill me with Your love.
Please lead me into a full understanding of Your love,
and keep me from choosing the wrong path. Amen.

Blessed Redeemer

*For God so loved the world that he gave his one and only Son,
that whoever believes in him shall not perish but have eternal life.*
JOHN 3:16 NIV

Compassion is "sympathetic consciousness of others' distress together with a desire to alleviate it" *(Merriam-Webster).* Oh, how our God loved us and showed His compassion. He knew we were a sinful people, and we were in peril. Our eternal lives were at stake. And He had a plan. He provided a way for redemption.

Despite the fact we did not deserve His unmerited favor, grace, He gave it to us anyway. He looked down on mankind and desired to bridge the separation between us. He sent His Son, Jesus, to die on the cross for our sins so we might live the resurrected life. Once we've accepted this free gift, we can rejoice!

We were in distress, and God came to the rescue. What a mighty God we serve! And how He loves us. The rescuing Shepherd came for His flock. He bore what we deserved because He had such compassion. True love, which our Father gives, is eternal. He loved us before we loved Him. What an amazing concept He desires us to grasp! Know today that your heavenly Father loves you.

*Dear Lord, how gracious and loving You are to me.
Thank You, Father, for Your arms about me this day. Amen.*

God-Things and God-Songs

I waited and waited and waited for GOD. At last he looked;
finally he listened. He lifted me out of the ditch, pulled
me from deep mud. He stood me up on a solid rock to
make sure I wouldn't slip. He taught me how to sing
the latest God-song, a praise-song to our God.
PSALM 40:1–3 MSG

When God alone teaches us how to worship, it is true and from the heart. Isaiah 30:20–21 (NLT) tells us that "Though the Lord gave you adversity for food and suffering for drink, he will still be with you to teach you. You will see your teacher with your own eyes. Your own ears will hear him. Right behind you a voice will say, 'This is the way you should go,' whether to the right or to the left."

God Himself wants to rescue you and to teach you. He alone is your Savior. No other human—as much as that person might try or intend to help you—can save you. If you allow Him, the God of heaven and earth will lift you up out of your despair and striving and set you free. He will teach you how to praise Him, even in the midst of suffering and trials. Quiet yourself before God and He will teach you.

God, I want to hear from You. Forgive me for wanting
others to rescue me. That is only Yours to do. Please
quiet my heart so that I can learn from You. Amen.

To Your Health!

*Dear friend, I hope all is well with you and that you
are as healthy in body as you are strong in spirit.*
3 JOHN 2 NLT

God cares about your health. He took the time to mention it in His Word
on multiple occasions. If you have any lingering doubts, just look at the
many, many times Jesus healed the sick. His heart always went out to those
who were struggling. With one touch, years of pain and agony disappeared.
Maybe you're like many women and struggle with your health. Perhaps
you're in chronic pain or live with an illness—diagnosed or undiagnosed.
Today, be reminded that God cares! He longs to see you living life to your
fullest potential. That same "touch" that healed the leper in Bible times is
still available today, and God is no respecter of persons. What He's done
for others He will do for you. Instead of giving in to fear (or thoughts that
you're alone), reach out to Him. He loves you and longs to heal both your
heart and body.

*Thank You, God, for caring about my health. It's such a relief to
know that You want me to be healthy, not just my heart and soul
but my body as well. I'm so grateful for Your healing, Father. Amen.*

Silent Fight

"The LORD will fight for you,
and you shall hold your peace."
EXODUS 14:14 NKJV

In this day and age when action is so heavily stressed, it is hard for us to wrap our heads around the thought of not acting. Is this truly what the Lord commands of us in times of struggle? Waiting on God's will and timing is one of the hardest acts.

We must remember God's might and power. He created the very atoms of the ground we tread, and if we are honest, there are many times we stomp around creating chaos in our lives when all we seek is order. The thought of ceasing from our plans and obeying God's will is frightening. We have an idea of the road God wishes us to walk and it's far outside our comfort zone. But then, think of the times we wrestled with His plan, gave in, and rejoiced in His work!

When God calls us to reach outside of ourselves and forgive or trust, it tears us from our selfish pride, rids us of embittered desires, and cleanses the channels of our hearts. We must trust that the most strenuous and arduous tasks God gives us will bear the most fruit and draw us closer to Him. To know that the God of the universe fights for us, undeserving sinners, leaves us astounded.

Father, thank You for listening to my prayers!
Thank You for never forsaking me even in the fight.
You are a great and gracious Father! Amen.

God's Gift

"I tell you, you can pray for anything, and if you believe that you've received it, it will be yours."

MARK 11:24 NLT

Notice the words in this verse. It says we're to believe we have received what we pray for. That's past tense. It doesn't take faith to believe our prayers will be answered after what we asked for is in plain sight. Trusting Him for answers before we see them is what the Lord wants.

The Bible tells us that without faith it is impossible to please God (see Hebrews 11:6). That may sound harsh, but scripture also promises that He gives each of us a measure of faith (see Romans 12:3).

If you gave your daughter a present and she left it on a shelf, unopened, you'd be disappointed. It may have been something she really wanted, so you found the perfect gift and wrapped it beautifully, but it is useless just sitting there. It's the same with God's gift of faith. We don't have to struggle with positive thinking or work up enough faith. All we have to do is accept what He has already provided and exercise the faith He gives.

Some people misuse this scripture and pray for foolish things that aren't according to His will. But when we stay close to Him, our desires will line up with His and we can have complete confidence that we will receive our request.

Dear Father, thank You for the faith You generously give me. I want my desires to perfectly align with Your desires for me so I can ask with true faith, knowing You have already provided the answer. Amen.

41

Game Plan

*Do not be anxious about anything, but in every situation,
by prayer and petition, with thanksgiving, present your requests
to God. And the peace of God, which transcends all understanding,
will guard your hearts and your minds in Christ Jesus.*
PHILIPPIANS 4:6–7 NIV

Do you find yourself being overly anxious at times? Is it hard to shut off the worrisome thoughts that crowd your mind? The enemy wants to fill you with fear and anxiety. His plan is to steal, kill, and destroy (see John 10:10), and that includes destroying your peace and thankfulness. But God's plan is that you have life and have it abundantly! So, how can you shut off the anxiety and worry to make room for the abundant life God has for you right here and now? Our gracious God has given us a game plan:

- Whenever you find yourself worried or anxious, stop to pray.
- Give thanks! Tell God your worries and ask Him to fill you with joy in His presence (see Psalm 16:11).
- When you do those things, the very peace of God. . .which doesn't make any sense to our human minds. . .will guard your heart and mind through Christ.

Through the ages, men and women of God have relied on this game plan to get them through unimaginable circumstances: Mothers losing a child to cancer have been given peace through the power of Christ. Soldiers held captive by the enemy have been filled with the presence of God. If you are struggling with an uncertain future, find rest and peace in Christ alone.

*God, I'm worried and afraid. Please fill me with Your peace in
this situation. Thank You for Your unfailing love! Amen.*

Open to God

*Open your mouth and taste, open your
eyes and see—how good GOD is.*
PSALM 34:8 MSG

Today's verse tells us that God wants us to experience Him with our physical senses. As we see the beauty of the world, as we taste a good meal, as we listen to the voices of our family members, as we feel the warmth of blankets on a frosty winter night, and as we breathe in the scent of a flower, we are experiencing the goodness of God.

"Open your mouths!" God tells us. "Listen! Keep your eyes open! I'm everywhere around you, waiting for you to experience Me." As we learn to perceive God with our bodies, we'll find our emotions tend to be more joyful and our spirits grow closer to Him.

The Living One is all around us, longing for us to experience His very being with every level of our own being. "Open your mouth and taste, open your eyes and see—how good GOD is"!

Today, God, I ask that You remind me to see You, to hear You, to taste You, to touch You, and even to smell You. As my body's senses are filled with You, fill also my heart and soul with Yourself.

Perfect Peace

*You will keep in perfect peace all who trust in you,
all whose thoughts are fixed on you! Trust in the
Lord always, for the Lord God is the eternal Rock.*
ISAIAH 26:3–4 NLT

What does perfect peace look like? Is it a life without problems? Is it a smooth ride into the future without any bumps in the road? Not for the Christian. We know life on earth won't ever be easy, but God promises to keep us in perfect peace if our thoughts are fixed on Him.

Perfect peace is only found by having a moment-by-moment relationship with Jesus Christ. It is ongoing faith and trust that God really has it all figured out. It's believing that each setback, heartbreak, problem, and crisis will be made right by God.

You can live in peace even during the messy stuff of life. You don't have to have everything figured out on your own. Doesn't that take some pressure off?

And the God of all grace, who called you to His eternal glory in Christ, after you have suffered a little while, will Himself restore you and make you strong, firm, and steadfast (1 Peter 5:10). That's perfect peace.

*Heavenly Father, thank You for offering me peace in the midst of
the stress of this life. Thank You that I'm not in charge and that
You have everything already figured out. I trust You. Amen.*

Peace of Heart —and Mind

Do not let your hearts be troubled (distressed, agitated).
JOHN 14:1 AMPC

Jesus not only tells you to not let your heart be troubled but also gives you reasons why you can stay calm, cool, and collected no matter what or who comes your way.

- Jesus says He's gone ahead of you to prepare a place for you in Father God's house. No need to ask for directions—you'll know how to get there (John 14:2–6).
- Jesus says that if you believe in Him, you will be able to do "even greater things" (John 14:12 AMPC).
- Jesus says He will do whatever you ask in His name (John 14:14).
- Jesus has asked God to send you the Holy Spirit, "another Comforter (Counselor, Helper, Intercessor, Advocate, Strengthener, and Standby), that He may remain with you forever" and live "with you [constantly] and. . .be in you" (John 14:16, 17 AMPC).

Can you feel the calm pouring over you?
No matter how rough life may seem, remember Jesus' calming words:

Peace I leave with you; My [own] peace I now give and bequeath to you. Not as the world gives do I give to you. Do not let your hearts be troubled, neither let them be afraid. [Stop allowing yourselves to be agitated and disturbed; and do not permit yourselves to be fearful and intimidated and cowardly and unsettled.]
JOHN 14:27 AMPC

Lord of peace, live in me. Keep my heart and mind—calm, cool, and collected—in You.

Expectant Living

All the creatures look expectantly to you to give them their meals on time. You come, and they gather around; you open your hand and they eat from it. If you turned your back, they'd die in a minute— take back your Spirit and they die, revert to original mud.

PSALM 104:27–29 MSG

What a beautiful reminder that we can look expectantly for God's provision. Think of how He meets the needs of nature and animals, so much so that it's an automatic assumption. The birds aren't stressed out. The grass isn't complaining. The deer don't worry about their next meal. They just know provision will come in one form or another. They embrace the ebbs and flows life brings their way with the seasons.

Let your faith in God be so strong that your actions display it. Let the promises throughout His Word sink so deep into the marrow of your bones that you live expectantly for His goodness. Let it be your automatic assumption when struggles arise.

Friend, the Lord's love for you is unending and unshakable. It's forever trustworthy. And when this truth becomes your operating system, it will affect the way you live your life. It'll guide you through every up and down.

Lord, thank You for seeing my every need and meeting each in meaningful ways. Give me the kind of faith that expects Your goodness to come to pass. Help me live without worry or fear no matter what comes—or doesn't come—my way.

Overwhelmed

*The cords of death entangled me, the anguish of the grave came over me; I was overcome by distress and sorrow. Then I called on the name of the L*ORD.

PSALM 116:3–4 NIV

Everyone feels overwhelmed at times. Perhaps we spill our morning coffee or we're late for work or we're facing a daunting task with seemingly no resolution or we've been betrayed by a close friend. Sometimes it feels as if Murphy's Law is the order of the day: "Anything that can go wrong, will go wrong." What we need to remember is we're not alone.

Even David had bad days, times when he experienced seemingly unbearable hardships. But when the chips were down, he did not lose faith. In Psalm 63:1–2, he writes, "You, God, are my God, earnestly I seek you; I thirst for you, my whole being longs for you, in a dry and parched land where there is no water. I have seen you in the sanctuary and beheld your power and your glory" (NIV).

Just as God cared for and protected David, He will care for and protect you too. David, just like you, faced many hardships—but rather than feel defeated, he used those struggles to make himself stronger. You too can emerge victorious in any difficulty by merely keeping the faith and calling on the name of the Lord.

Dear God, guide me through difficult times, strengthen me, and help me to learn from every experience.

Loved and Valued

*Then Jacob went on his way,
and God's angels met him.*
GENESIS 32:1 AMPC

You may not be a patriarch, a male, a father, a big name in the annals of history. But you are just as important in God's eyes as Jacob was. So it stands to reason that as you go on your way with God, there are angels surrounding you, reassuring you of God's presence and theirs, protecting you from dangers seen and unseen.

In fact, the Bible says that very thing! Because you have made God your refuge, He commands His angels to guard you (Psalm 91:9–12).

Jesus makes a point in telling His followers that not one little sparrow falls to the ground without God knowing about it. In fact, says He, every hair on each believer's head is numbered. "So don't be afraid; you are more valuable to God than a whole flock of sparrows" (Matthew 10:31 NLT).

That's how much God is aware of you. That's how much He loves you. That's how much He values you.

So the next time you find yourself overwhelmed with thoughts of worry and worthlessness, when your fear threatens to override your faith, remember all those angels and the Lord of light with you—loving you, guarding you, looking out for you. And soon you and your mind will be set back on the right light-filled course.

You, Lord, are my refuge, my love, my life, and light!

Time to Love God

But do not forget this one thing, dear friends:
With the Lord a day is like a thousand years,
and a thousand years are like a day.

2 PETER 3:8 NIV

"The time is just flying by."

"I don't have time."

"There aren't enough hours in a day."

Surely you've heard those words. You've probably said them yourself. In today's busy world, there just doesn't seem to be enough time. People communicate instantaneously. They work quickly, play fast, and live by tight schedules. Even when they pray, they expect God to answer quickly. But God doesn't work that way. The Bible says that to Him a thousand years are like a day.

God's patience toward us is a reflection of His love. There are many examples of His loving patience in the Bible, but the best is His patience with the Israelites. Psalm 78:41 (NLT) says, "Again and again they tested God's patience." Still, God continued to love them, and His patience with Israel exists to this day.

Patience requires time, and although it is not infinite, God's patience is immense. He allows people time to know Him, to trust Him, and to believe in His Son and the gift of salvation. He gives them a lifetime in which to do it and, after that, the promise of eternal life with Him in heaven. Now, that's true love!

Dear God, help me to love others patiently,
the same way that You love me. Amen.

Read, Heed, and Lead

Listen to the words of the wise; apply your heart to my instruction. For it is good to keep these sayings in your heart and always ready on your lips.
PROVERBS 22:17–18 NLT

A great way to keep your mind focused on the positive, your heart tender, and your actions good is to "listen to the words of the wise." And where will you find such words? In the Bible, the bestselling book of all time as of 1995, according to *Guinness World Records*.

Read and then heed the words of God. Allow them to guide you through life. Spend time memorizing what you read, especially the verses that truly move you. Storing such words up in your heart during times of contentment will serve to keep you calm during times of chaos. When the stinging words of others or your own discouraging thoughts threaten your peace of mind, being able to recite God's words aloud will be a balm to not just your spirit and soul but to others who hear God's spoken wisdom.

So remember to read God's Word, heed His wisdom, and allow both to lead your heart and mind to a better place.

Bring to my attention, Lord, those words of wisdom You'd like me to store in my heart. Then show me ways in which I can incorporate those words into my life to Your glory and my peace. In Jesus' name I pray, amen.

The Path

"Come to me, all who labor and are heavy laden, and I will give you rest. Take my yoke upon you, and learn from me, for I am gentle and lowly in heart, and you will find rest for your souls."
Matthew 11:28–29 esv

Jesus shows you His path of life by giving you the formula for how to live it.

The first step is to go to Jesus, to enter into His presence—not when you're in a rush nor with the attitude that spending time with Him is just one more thing to check off your list. He wants you to truly seek Him out with all your heart.

The second step is to learn to live as Jesus lived, walk as He walked, do as He did. As you do so, you will become as gentle and humble in your heart as He. Following His pathway, taking those steps, will bring rest, renewal, and peace to your soul.

As you live in and walk closer to Jesus, as you model His mode of living, you'll find yourself saying, "I will bless the Lord who guides me; even at night my heart instructs me. I know the Lord is always with me. I will not be shaken, for he is right beside me" (Psalm 16:7–8 nlt).

Lord, "You make known to me the path of life; in your presence there is fullness of joy. . .pleasures forevermore" (Psalm 16:11 esv).

The Balm of a Psalm

The Lord is my shepherd; I have all that I need.
He lets me rest in green meadows; he leads me beside
peaceful streams. He renews my strength. He guides
me along right paths, bringing honor to his name.
PSALM 23:1–3 NLT

Psalm 23 is the most well-known and beloved psalm in the Bible, a balm to many souls—and there's a good reason for that.

When you feel lost, alone, and afraid, David's psalm assures you that God, your shepherd, is with you. And because He is, you will not lack. For He will lead you to rest in fresh green pastures, guide you to soothing still water. He'll restore your strength and lead you down the right road.

Psalm 23 reminds you that when you walk through the dark valleys, you need have no thought of fear because God is with you, carrying a rod to protect you and a staff to guide you. He'll prepare a feast for you in the presence of your enemies, revive your sagging head, and fill your cup full of blessings.

Because God is with you and will always be with you, His goodness and love will follow you wherever you go.

When your mind is on overload, your heart trembling, your spirit drooping, sink yourself into this psalm, the balm for your soul.

Lord, You are my shepherd. . . .

Still Before the Lord

Be still and rest in the Lord; wait for Him and patiently lean yourself upon Him; fret not yourself because of him who prospers in his way, because of the man who brings wicked devices to pass. Cease from anger and forsake wrath; fret not yourself—it tends only to evildoing.
PSALM 37:7–8 AMPC

We often can't control our emotional reactions to life's challenges and disappointments. We can, however, choose how we handle those emotions, making an active effort to entrust them, as well as any thoughts that spurred them, to the Lord. One way to do this is to sit silently in God's presence, turning each thought over to Him as it enters our minds.

By making this practice a habit, we will gradually learn to be still before the Lord—and then, as we go through our day, instead of fretting and worrying, we can continue this practice of releasing each negative thought into God's care.

As Martin Luther once said, "You cannot keep birds from flying over your head but you can keep them from building a nest in your hair."

I give the details of my life to You, Lord, as well as my emotions. Remind me not to whine and agonize over life's complications. Teach me to catch myself when I'm doing that—and then immediately turn my frustration, anger, and fears over to You. Help me keep those negative emotions from building nests in my hair!

Be Still and Learn

His delight and desire are in the law of the Lord, and on His law (the precepts, the instructions, the teachings of God) he habitually meditates (ponders and studies) by day and by night.
PSALM 1:2 AMPC

Do you desire to know God better? To be strengthened by Him? Spending time with the Lord in prayer and Bible reading are the best ways to learn more about His mercy, His kindness, His love, and His peace.

These disciplines are like water on a sponge. They help us understand who God is and what He brings to our lives. In His presence, we become aware of His blessings and the resources He has provided to strengthen us for each day's battles. He will empower us to fulfill His plan for our lives.

It does take discipline to spend time with the Lord, but that simple discipline helps to keep our hope alive, providing light for our paths. When the schedule seems to loom large or the weariness of everyday living tempts you to neglect prayer and Bible study—remember they are your lifeline. They keep you growing in your relationship with the Lover of your soul.

Heavenly Father, I want to know You more. I want to feel Your presence. Teach me Your ways that I may dwell in the house of the Lord forever. Amen.

The Authority of Jesus

Jesus. . .said to them, All authority (all power of rule) in heaven and on earth has been given to Me. Go then and make disciples of all the nations, . . .teaching them to observe everything that I have commanded you, and behold, I am with you all the days (perpetually, uniformly, and on every occasion), to the [very] close and consummation of the age.

MATTHEW 28:18–20 AMPC

It seems as though each day brings bad news—a new act of violence, another natural disaster, or one more political controversy. We don't have to be ostriches, though, burying our heads in the sand so we don't see what's happening around us.

Jesus calls us to have confidence in His authority at work in the world, regardless of circumstances. He asks us to participate in His mission, helping people learn about Him and His love. As we take action for Jesus, we can rest in the knowledge that no matter what is happening in our world, He is with us.

Thank You, Jesus, that You are right beside me in every situation. Give me the strength I need to be Your hands and feet, Your smile and touch, Your voice and ears to each person I encounter today. May I carry with me the constant awareness of Your authority and love.

Because He's God!

Let those on the hunt for you sing and celebrate. Let all who love your saving way say over and over, "God is mighty!"
PSALM 70:4 MSG

David is calling all God's people to be happy in Him and to sing His praises. He doesn't put any stipulations on it: "*If* God makes your life perfect. . ." or "*If* God answers your prayers the way you'd like Him to. . ." or "*If* God blesses you financially. . ." There are no "ifs"—no requirements are attached to David's directive. God's people should be joyful solely *because He's God!*

Today, let your thoughts rest on the character of God. He is good. He is holy. He is just. He is infinite. He is patient. He is faithful. He is love. He is forgiving. He is creative. He is truth. He is welcoming. . .and so much more! Spend some time in His Word, and you'll realize that God is worthy of your love and praise just because of who He is.

When you focus on how good God is (all the time!), you'll find your heart growing more grateful, more content, more joyful. And when your heart is overflowing with joy, positivity will trickle into every area of your life. Say it out loud: "God is mighty!"

God, You are mighty! You are so, so good to me. I am so grateful to have You in my heart and in my life. I praise You! Amen.

The Spirit's Power

I came to you in weakness with great fear and trembling.
My message and my preaching were not with wise and persuasive
words, but with a demonstration of the Spirit's power, so that
your faith might not rest on human wisdom, but on God's power.
1 CORINTHIANS 2:3–5 NIV

Have you ever had to stand up to speak to a group of people and felt your knees knocking together? Perhaps a bead of sweat started rolling down your back as well. Maybe your hands got cold and clammy. Yet still, something urged you on. Something gave you the power to open your mouth and speak. That was a demonstration of the Spirit's power. And because of that power, your faith rests in God, not in you and your human wisdom.

Psalm 125:1 (NIV) says, "Those who trust in the LORD are like Mount Zion, which cannot be shaken but endures forever." When the going gets tough, when your knees start wobbling, remember God is in control. Let your faith in God render you unshakable and be at peace, knowing He is at the helm, steering you to calmer shores.

Dear God, be my eyes, ears, and mind. Through You, I trust that
my path is as it should be. Guide me safely through each day.

Building Your House

*By wisdom a house is built, and through understanding
it is established; through knowledge its rooms are
filled with rare and beautiful treasures.*

PROVERBS 24:3–4 NIV

As a woman, you play an important role in the lives of those closest to you. You represent the Lord and serve as a role model to those around you. You are an example every single day. You build a reputation over time, and your family and friends learn what matters most to you through your reactions to life's circumstances, both the blessings and the trials.

When a house is built, it must stand on a firm foundation. If your life is built upon the foundation of faith, it will shine before others and provide strength for them as well.

Resist the urge to focus on the outward and be content with less than those around you materially. True treasures are not found through online shopping but by tapping into the power source of your Lord and Savior.

Seek the wisdom of the Father through His holy Word and through prayer. Associate with other believers in the Christian community. Find time to rest and set yourself apart from the busy, busy, busy of this world. These things will help you to establish a house built with wisdom as its basis.

Lord, may I build my life upon a foundation of faith in You.

Keep the Peace

*You will guard him and keep him in perfect and constant peace
whose mind [both its inclination and its character] is stayed
on You, because he commits himself to You, leans on You, and
hopes confidently in You. So trust in the Lord (commit yourself
to Him, lean on Him, hope confidently in Him) forever; for
the Lord God is an everlasting Rock [the Rock of Ages].*
ISAIAH 26:3–4 AMPC

When your peace of mind and heart has flown out the window, Isaiah gives you some steps to get it back. First, remember that God is the guardian of your peace. Second, remember that your calm can be recaptured if you fix your thoughts on the Lord. Third, remember that He is the only one worthy of your trust.

Then you, like Paul, will find that even if you have "conflicts on the outside, fears inside" (2 Corinthians 7:5 HCSB), you will find the calm you crave from "God, who comforts the humble" (2 Corinthians 7:6 HCSB). Then, with the peace and calm from God, you will find yourself to be a person "close to his heart" (Psalm 148:14 NIV), praising "the name of the LORD, for his name alone is exalted; his majesty is above earth and heaven" (Psalm 148:13 ESV).

*Heavenly Father, thanks for being the guardian of
my heart peace, the calmer of my mind. In this moment,
I fix my thoughts on You—the Lord I trust and lean on!*

Gracious Spirit

*Answer me quickly, Lord; my spirit fails. Don't hide
Your face from me, or I will be like those going down to the
Pit. Let me experience Your faithful love in the morning,
for I trust in You. Reveal to me the way I should go because
I long for You. Rescue me from my enemies, Lord; I come to
You for protection. Teach me to do Your will, for You are my
God. May Your gracious Spirit lead me on level ground.*
PSALM 143:7–10 HCSB

David prayed to God for answers. He prayed for God's loving presence, help, protection, wisdom, and knowledge. He prayed for the grace of the Spirit to lead and guide him.

David's humble pleas revealed just how much he wanted his thoughts, heart, and actions to line up with God's and His call on His life.

Maybe David's words resonate with you. Perhaps today, you are looking to God for an answer, for more of His presence and wisdom, for the power of the Holy Spirit to move in your life and the lives of others, for the Lord's grace to abound, to lead you to level ground.

In this moment, take some time to quiet your mind, heart, and body through prayer. Let God's gracious Spirit touch you in a way that shows you just how precious you—a dearly loved daughter of the King—are.

Gracious God, I come to You now. I need Your wisdom and presence.

Morning Joy

*Sing the praises of the LORD, you his faithful people;
praise his holy name. For his anger lasts only a moment,
but his favor lasts a lifetime; weeping may stay for
the night, but rejoicing comes in the morning.*

PSALM 30:4–5 NIV

During our hardest trials, the nights are long. When we toss and turn and can't sleep. . . When we can't stop the tears from falling. . . When our minds race with negative thoughts. . . When we don't have the words or even the energy to pray. . . When it seems like our world will never be made right again. . . There is hope because God's Word promises that morning will come! And with the new morning comes hope! And hope will always come because of Jesus.

Although we may not have a smooth and easy road ahead, our loving heavenly Father is beside us every step of the way. And, if we stick close to Him, He offers us His favor. He promises that joy will come again—despite the pain and sorrow we're experiencing in the moment.

So, like the psalmist, offer your sincerest praise. Thank the heavenly Father for His love. Thank Him for His promises. Thank Him for new mornings of rejoicing after long, sleepless nights.

*Lord, thank You for Your favor. You are so good to me.
Although You don't promise me a life free from hardship
and pain, You do promise hope and joy.*

Remembering His Promises

*Tell everyone about God's power. His majesty shines
down on Israel; his strength is mighty in the heavens.
God is awesome in his sanctuary. The God of Israel gives
power and strength to his people. Praise be to God!*

PSALM 68:34–35 NLT

Do you ever find yourself dreaming of a place of safety? A place where you can close your eyes, rest your head, and let go of the stress and angst that follow you around like a shadow? It rarely matters what kind of season you are in—busy or calm—you always seem to feel an inner longing to find a place where there is nothing but peace.

Before you move on to the next thing on the list, take a moment to close your eyes. Don't reach for a book. Refuse to look at your phone. Keep your thoughts from wandering away. And simply fix your heart on the one who loves you. Think about His compassion. Dwell on His promises. Consider His majesty and the army of angels He commands. Have faith in the one He sent so you can forever be with Him.

Whether you need comfort, encouragement, or protection, He is the answer. Look first in His direction for clarity and understanding. He is close at hand and forever unchanging.

*Lord, thank You for showing me that You are my everything.
Through every day, through every year, I need only to fix
my eyes on You—the author and perfecter of my faith.*

Have Thine Own Way

Know that the LORD is God. It is he who made us, and we
are his; we are his people, the sheep of his pasture.
PSALM 100:3 NIV

"Thou art the potter, I am the clay." Those are ringing words from the song "Have Thine Own Way" that stirs up emotions and a desire to allow God to mold us and make us in His image. But what a hard thing to do. We strive to create our own worlds, to make a plan, to fix it. However, God asks us to allow Him free rein.

Sheep follow their shepherd and trust in him for provision. "As in thy presence humbly I bow." Submissive to their masters, they quietly graze the hillsides knowing the shepherd knows best. What a wonderfully relaxing word picture: relying on God's guidance and timing, following His lead.

It is a simple prayer to ask Him to help us give up control, yet not a simple task. In obedience to His word, we can bow our heads and ask for the Holy Spirit's direction and take our hands from the steering wheel. Then wait. Quietly on our hillsides, not champing at the bit; hearts "yielded and still." We wait for the still, small voice. This day, resolve to listen and follow.

Lord, we humbly bow before You and ask for Your divine
guidance. Help us to follow Your plan with yielded
hearts, ever ready to give up control to You. Amen.

Looking beyond Earthly Reassurances

Some nations boast of their chariots and horses,
but we boast in the name of the LORD our God.
PSALM 20:7 NLT

David, the writer of this psalm, did not find his hope in things that came from this earth—things he could see with his own eyes or create with his own hands. He did not find it through a solution his mind could conjure. He had faith in the Lord, and that was enough. We can only imagine how comforting it would be to look upon our defending army during a time of war, but he chose to look beyond the army and instead fixed his eyes on the Lord.

Through any trial or pain, the Lord sees all, and He loves His people in a deep, unfailing way. Although a thousand may fall, our fate and lives rest in Him and Him alone. We cannot look to earthly things to predict our future, finances, employment, etc. God's plans far exceed anything we could plan, and if we trust and follow Him, we will end up in a place we never would have come up with on our own.

Breathe in. Breathe out. Rest and believe. It is through fixing our eyes on God and looking to Him for direction that we are reassured and can experience peace.

Lord, please set my eyes on You. Help me not to seek
reassurance through earthly things but to understand on
a deeper level that You control all. You hold my heart and
care about each step I take. My hope is in You alone.

My Morning Prayer

Let me hear Your faithfulness in the morning;
for I trust in You; teach me the way in which I
should walk; for to You I lift up my soul.
PSALM 143:8 NASB

Do mornings excite or depress you? "Good morning, Lord!" or "Good Lord, it's morning!" When David wrote Psalm 143, he probably dreaded the sun coming up because that meant his enemies could continue pursuing him and persecuting his soul. "The enemy. . .has crushed my life to the ground" (verse 3 NASB). "My spirit feels weak within me; my heart is appalled" (verse 4 NASB).

What did David do when he didn't know which way to turn? He turned to the Lord. He stayed in prayer contact with God and meditated on God's faithfulness and righteousness (verse 1), God's past work in his life (verse 5), and His loyal love (verses 8, 12). He also took refuge in God (verse 9) and continued serving Him (verse 12).

No matter what our day holds, we can face it confidently by practicing verse 8. Let's look for God's loving-kindness and keep trusting Him no matter what. Ask Him to teach and lead us in the way He wants us to go. We have the privilege of offering up our souls (thoughts, emotions, and will) to Him anew each morning. Have a good day.

Good morning, Lord. You are my loving Father, secure refuge,
and trustworthy God. Deliver me from my enemies and show
me Your loving heart as I trust in You. Help me to please You
today in my decisions and goals, in my attitudes toward
circumstances, and in the way I respond to people around me.

Contentment

Don't be obsessed with getting more material things.
Be relaxed with what you have. Since God assured us,
"I'll never let you down, never walk off and leave you,"
we can boldly quote, God is there, ready to help;
I'm fearless no matter what. Who or what can get to me?
HEBREWS 13:5–6 MSG

We all want to understand. Understand why bad things happen. Understand why certain decisions get made. Understand why grace was given to us when we didn't deserve it. We all want to understand what God is up to in our life.

Proverbs 20:24 (NLT) asks, "The LORD directs our steps, so why try to understand everything along the way?"

If we trust in God—that He is for us, loves us, and is in control of our lives—then trying to analyze or understand everything won't be something that consumes us. Instead, contentment can consume us. All of this sounds easier said than done, right? It happens through a process called *sanctification*. Sanctification occurs over time as the Holy Spirit works in our lives to mold us into the likeness of Jesus.

So when you have those moments where you become obsessed with trying to figure things out, stop, take a few deep breaths, and say out loud, "God, I trust You! I choose to be content!"

Abba Father, more than anything in this life I desire
contentment in You. For that's where I find peace
and trust that I can't explain or understand.

Stilling Storms

He got up and rebuked the winds and the sea, and there was
a great and wonderful calm (a perfect peaceableness).
And the men were stunned with bewildered wonder
and marveled, saying, What kind of Man is this,
that even the winds and the sea obey Him!
MATTHEW 8:26–27 AMPC

Wanting to get a break from the crowds of people surrounding Him, Jesus got into a boat. The disciples followed Him and headed out across the lake.

Suddenly, a storm came upon them. The wind and waves became so violent that the boat began filling with water. But Jesus was in the stern, sleeping. In a panic, His disciples woke Jesus, pleading for Him to save them.

After admonishing His followers for having so little faith and so much fear, Jesus arose and scolded the wind and waves. At once, there was a great calm—a "perfect peaceableness."

Your Lord Jesus has power over the storms within and without. Making this a certainty in your mind should keep your fear from stressing your faith. Simply take it as a fact that with Jesus in the stern of your boat, there's no place for panic. That all you need to do is stay calm, for He won't let anything harm you—no matter how big the waves, how strong the current, how violent the wind.

Thank You, Lord, for stilling the storms inside and outside of me!

The Sanctuary

I have seen you in the sanctuary and beheld your power
and your glory.... I will praise you as long as I live.
PSALM 63:2, 4 NIV

As David—the shepherd, warrior, then king—continued to wander in the desert, he wasn't alone. God was with him. As David was on the run—praising, weeping, and wandering—he recalled the glimpse he'd had of God's glory in the tent of meeting.

In the Old Testament, God promised to be present with His people within the confines of a tabernacle. But David knew God could never truly be tied to the inside of a building. David knew the Lord was with him, as was His glorious power and strength.

Because of Jesus, God's daughters have the chance to access that divine power and strength any moment they need it. Your heart and soul are now the sanctuary where the glory of the Lord lives. God wants you to tap into that power every day by communicating with Him through prayer, by basking in His presence, by studying Him, by praising Him for as long as you live. The moment you are at your weakest, God will step from that sanctuary within you and show you His ultimate power.

Protector, thank You for always being with me as I seek Your peace
and presence through prayer, praise, study, and silence. Amen.

Thank You, Lord

I will praise the LORD at all times;
I will constantly speak his praises.

PSALM 34:1 NLT

While imprisoned, the apostle Paul gave thanks to God, even singing His praises, and it resulted in the salvation of the jailers. What a great lesson for every Christian—when you feel least like giving thanks, that's precisely when you should!

What is your response when you find yourself trapped in traffic, late for a meeting, frustrated in your plans, sick in bed, hurting emotionally, overwhelmed with work, lonely, tired, or confused? Our human nature teaches us that we should gripe and fret. Yet, scripture says we should give thanks. Only when we surrender our lives to Him and His control is this possible.

Learn to thank Him. Thank Him for being your help in time of trouble. Thank Him for His great wisdom and power. And thank Him for causing every situation in your life to work together for your good.

Giving thanks may not change your circumstances significantly, but it will change you. You'll feel yourself focusing on God—His goodness, kindness, and grace—rather than your own anger, pride, sickness, or inconvenience. Maybe that's why it's such fertile soil for miracles. The biblical commentator Matthew Henry stated it well: "Thanksgiving is good, but thanks-living is better."

Lord, I choose to give You thanks today for whatever comes my way. I love You, Lord, and I am grateful for Your goodness. Amen.

The Power of Praise

*Oh, let me sing to God all my life long, sing hymns to my God
as long as I live! Oh, let my song please him; I'm so pleased
to be singing to God. But clear the ground of sinners—no
more godless men and women! O my soul, bless God!*

PSALM 104:33–35 MSG

If you're busy singing praises to God, it's a surefire way to keep your
thoughts on the right things. Rather than obsessing over what disrespect-
ful words she said to you or wondering if you looked silly at the event or
trying to make sense of the fight you had with your spouse before work,
train your mind to focus on God's goodness.

Thanking Him has a unique way of changing our mood. It brings
a hopeful perspective when we need it the most. It shifts our negative
thoughts to positive ones as we remember His faithfulness in the hard
moments. And it keeps our eyes on the prize—eternity with God.

Be intentional to fill your mind with the joys of the Lord. Don't let anything in this world pull you from meditating on the Lord's magnificence.
Because when your thoughts are full of Him, your choices will follow.

*Lord, when my heart is heavy with the worries of the world,
help me remember all the times You've come through for me.
Lead me to praise and thank You. Help me focus on Your
provision, healing, and kindness so I can find peace.*

The Hopeful Wait

We wait in hope for the LORD; he is our help and our shield.
In him our hearts rejoice, for we trust in his holy name. May your
unfailing love be with us, LORD, even as we put our hope in you.
PSALM 33:20–22 NIV

So often, our waiting times are full of stress and anxiety. We wait and worry. . .we worry and wait. And the waiting is made even more difficult when our minds are overflowing with irritating, anxiety-inducing "what if" thoughts like:

What if I lose my job?
What if my friend won't forgive me?
What if I end up alone?
What if my future doesn't go as planned?

Waiting doesn't often feel hopeful, does it? . . . Is there even such a thing as "hopeful waiting"? . . . The answer, according to God's Word, is *yes*!

Whatever you're waiting for, God is a constant hope. You can trust Him because He's got everything under control. He sees all. He hears all. He knows all. And if that's not enough to ease your worried mind, He is our shield of protection. . .and His love is unfailing!

So, dear one, rejoice! Receive His protection. Welcome His love. In the most difficult waiting season, He will come to your rescue!

Father God, I will take heart as I wait. Thank You
for rescuing me, even in the most difficult seasons
of life. I will put my hope and trust in You alone!

"Be Still" Means Stop Striving

God is our refuge and strength, an ever-present help in trouble.
PSALM 46:1 NIV

News broadcasts distress us daily. We may be living in the time of "wars and rumors of wars" that Jesus predicted in Matthew 24:6. He added, "See to it that you are not alarmed. Such things must happen, but the end is still to come" (NIV). Because God is our refuge (fortress) and strength, we need not fear. Even when natural disasters strike (Psalm 46:2–3). Even during national conflicts (46:6). Note the refrain in verses 7 and 11 (NLT): "The LORD of Heaven's Armies is here among us." *Who could defend us better?* "The God of Israel [our personal God] is our fortress." *What better protection could we have?* God is also working to end all wars (46:8–9). He will win and be exalted in the end (46:10), which is sure to come.

In light of this, how should we respond? When verse 10 tells the nations to be still and know He is God, it means they should stop striving, lay down their arms. God will do the fighting and will eventually end all conflicts. Isaiah 2 is a parallel passage that describes the latter days when metal will be used for farming and fishing tools, not for weapons.

We can personalize this psalm by remembering to let God fight our battles. Stop striving and know that He is God, our refuge and strength.

Almighty God, I run to You for refuge. I depend on You for strength. Help me to stop fighting for my rights and let You be God! I rest in You.

Eternally Secure

For I am convinced that neither death, nor life, nor angels,
nor principalities, nor things present, nor things to come, nor powers,
nor height, nor depth, nor any other created thing, will be able to
separate us from the love of God that is in Christ Jesus our Lord.
ROMANS 8:38–39 NASB

In this life we often feel we need to work for love. Love can grow stale or be lost altogether or given to another. The promise of love can be used as a weapon against us. But in this verse, an eternal, genuine love is promised you. This promise can be trusted because the love of God has been secured through the sacrifice and death of Christ. This is no promise made on a whim or as a manipulation but one made in blood by the perfect Lamb.

No natural or supernatural power can separate you from God's love. Nothing that is currently happening in your life will separate you from God's love. No matter how scary or uncertain the future seems, it will not separate you from God's love. No height of success or depth of depression and despair will separate you from God's love. Nothing that this life and those in it can throw at you and nothing that you do will separate you from God's love. Not even death, which separates us from everything else we know, will separate you from God's love.

Therefore, go forward in peace and boldness, knowing that you are eternally secure and eternally loved.

Lord, I can't comprehend this kind of everlasting love, but I thank
You that I can rest in the promise that You will always love me.

Keeping Up with the Christian Joneses

"Come to Me, all you who labor and are
heavy laden, and I will give you rest."
MATTHEW 11:28 NKJV

Christians have a lot to do. There are so many needs in the world, from spreading the gospel and feeding the poor to teaching children the Bible and remaining in prayer.

But somehow, our practice of the faith has morphed into a jam-packed schedule of women's meetings, Christian sporting events, and committees. It's almost an unwritten rule that good Christian people must load their schedules with good Christian stuff to do, especially during the holidays.

With all the hurrying around, the precious limited time we have each day isn't allocated toward the actual works of God. It's taken up with busyness.

Consequently, our families are strangers, our hearts are unfulfilled, our minds are stressed, and our Bible reading and prayer life are shallow.

God isn't impressed with a clean house or schedules marked with every church event for the next six months. He wants our hearts, minds, and souls, and He wants us to be obedient to share His love with all people throughout our lives. It's not complicated.

If you find yourself unable to keep up with the fast-paced Christian life, then be at peace and say no sometimes. What really matters is the condition of our hearts.

Lord, help me see the difference between the life
of a Christian and the heart of a Christian, and
help me discern when my life is misaligned.

Unchangeable

*LORD, hear my prayer! Listen to my plea! Don't turn away
from me in my time of distress. Bend down to listen, and
answer me quickly when I call to you.... [The Lord] will
listen to the prayers of the destitute. He will not reject their
pleas.... You are always the same; you will live forever.*
PSALM 102:1–2, 17, 27 NLT

The world changes so quickly around us—places, faces, technology, relationships, mores, values, wars, boundaries, battles, surrenders, earthquakes, hurricanes, fires, and famine.... We can barely keep pace. Some days, we find ourselves breathless, not knowing what's sure and certain. We find ourselves feeling untethered, doubting the permanence of the very ground beneath our feet.

Yet, we're believers in a God who never changes. He's always ready to help, teach, correct, and save. He's the one place we know we can go when we have problems and pleas. He's the one person who'll never turn from us when we're in distress.

Pray. And know that when you do, God will bend His ear. Know that He'll find coherence in your babbling. Know that He'll never reject you—but protect you.

In this world of constant change, remember that you're enveloped by the permanence of your rock and refuge, standing on Him and trusting in Him alone.

*I pray to the unchangeable source and Lord of my
heart and life, knowing You will hear and answer.*

Are You Aware of Stress?

*You will keep in perfect peace all who trust in
you, all whose thoughts are fixed on you!*
ISAIAH 26:3 NLT

I suppose there aren't enough months in the year to focus on all our ailments and national concerns, so the calendar-makers piggyback them to give everyone a fair hearing. Are you ready for this? April is also Stress Awareness Month. And as you might guess, during this month, health care professionals try to increase awareness of the causes and cures for what is called our "modern stress epidemic."

We're all aware that stress is widespread and affects us in many ways. And stress management is difficult to implement. Taking a vacation only helps a few weeks out of the year. Relaxing on the weekend only increases the anxiety of Monday morning. Displaying beachfronts on our computer desktops only reminds us that we are office bound. And talking with a therapist is only a release valve for continuing pressure. Yes, stress is a problem, and it is here to stay.

For Christians, stress seems to fly in the face of Jesus' promise of peace and abundant joy. Yet, the peace He gives keeps the stress from destroying us. He keeps the threads of our sanity from unraveling. But He expects us to do what we can to help ourselves. This month, take a good look at your schedule and your routines and ask God for wisdom so you can appropriately manage your stress.

*God, grant me the serenity to accept the things
I cannot change, courage to change the things
I can, and wisdom to know the difference.*

Focusing on Today

*Don't brag about tomorrow, since you
don't know what the day will bring.*
PROVERBS 27:1 NLT

What do you have on your plate today? What about tomorrow? Do you remember those plans you have next week? And that trip you have later this month? What about the work thing you have next year?

If we take an honest look at this verse, we see there is no point in worrying about tomorrow, just as there is no point in worrying about next year! *Nothing* is set in stone. Even today is a fluid river of moments, susceptible to change.

We will find that we can be happier in life by simply taking each day as it comes. If we are not focused on our calendar of events, and instead decidedly focused on each moment of *this* day, we will have the ability to enjoy moments that otherwise would have passed us by. The hilarious thing your child just said that bubbles into laughter. The sweet message from your husband that warms your heart. A lunch date with a friend that encourages your soul. These are all moments we can revel in and enjoy rather than thinking about the next thing on the list or schedule.

Today, let's keep our focus on only the events of *today*. We will find fulfillment, laughter, and a reduction in stress if we refuse to borrow the worries of tomorrow.

*Lord, thank You for encouraging me to live life moment by moment.
Help me to recognize the blessings that abound in each day.*

The Plan

For in You, O Lord, do I hope; You will answer, O Lord my God.
PSALM 38:15 AMPC

Say the words of this Psalm out loud. Do you have this kind of unwavering hope? Do you *really* believe God hears and will answer?

If you've ever put your hope in a human relationship, odds are you were let down at some point. You were disappointed by a broken promise. Or things just didn't go quite like you had planned. The problem is that just as in our human relationships, we often put our very limited human expectations on God. And then, when He does things His way (and not ours), we feel let down. We're disappointed. *We had a plan, after all, and God didn't stick to it! . . .*

The difference is that humans are imperfect. They're selfish. And they don't always look out for our well-being. But we can trust that when God doesn't do things our way, it's for good reason. Because He knows what's truly best for us. So, we can always hope in His plan. We can wholeheartedly trust that He will answer at the right time. And whatever His plan, it's perfect!

"For I know the plans I have for you," says the LORD.
"They are plans for good. . .to give you a future and a hope."
JEREMIAH 29:11 NLT

God, I'm sorry for all the times I've put my limited human expectations on You. You are my hope, and I trust You!

The Lord Made This Day

This is the day the LORD has made;
we will rejoice and be glad in it.
PSALM 118:24 NKJV

Renee hated dark, overcast days without any sunshine. She felt lethargic and depressed on those days. She avoided looking out the windows too much on cloudy, cold days, the gray sky a constant reminder the sun was hiding from her. After the colorful, cheerful celebration of Christmas, the dull drabness of January seemed to last forever. She felt like curling up somewhere and sleeping until winter passed. She could hardly wait for spring to arrive, but wishing didn't take away her dismal feelings or change the seasons.

As Christians, we don't have to feel depressed because it's a dark, wintry day. We can rejoice because we know God made this day and is in charge in spite of the gray skies overhead. If we only had sunshine in our lives, how would we know the way God can work to make each day a blessing even when there are gray skies overhead?

Sometimes, even when the sun is shining, our world looks cloudy because of some unpleasant task or trial. Christians aren't exempt from the dark, but we don't have to live there. Each day can be brightened by God's presence in our lives reminding us that He made the day and we can be glad about it.

Lord, help me to see past gray skies and
find the light of Your love in my life.

Laughing at the Days to Come

She is clothed with strength and dignity;
she can laugh at the days to come.
PROVERBS 31:25 NIV

You mean a woman of God can laugh at the days to come? Really? . . . Most of the world wakes up each morning under a black cloud of regret and a debilitating fear of the future. That sounds more realistic, right? To laugh at the future is hard to imagine. To see hope instead of futility? Promise in the pain? What would that kind of woman look like? Sound like?

Perhaps a woman of God as described in Proverbs 31 doesn't necessarily have a lot of confidence in herself but rather in God. Perhaps she trusts so implicitly in His divine plan and goodness that she can sleep deeply. She can wake up refreshed each morning.

And this woman of God knows some truths—that God will indeed work everything for good in her life. That He is watching over her comings and goings, and nothing will befall her that He can't handle. She knows that this earthly life is temporary. That heaven is not only for real but forever. Knowing these truths all the way to her soul gives her peace and joy, and it shows in her countenance. Yes, and even in her laugh.

Jesus, help me trust in You every hour of every day, and let me be
so full of peace that I, too, can laugh at the days to come. Amen.

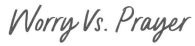

Worry Vs. Prayer

Don't worry about anything; instead,
pray about everything. Tell God what you need,
and thank him for all he has done.

PHILIPPIANS 4:6 NLT

Do not worry. This is a tall order for women. We are worriers by nature, aren't we? We worry about our children and friends. We worry about what people think of us and what we will do if such-and-such happens. We are the queens of the what-if's!

But the Bible tells us not to worry about *anything*. In the book of Matthew, we are reminded that if God cares for the birds of the air, providing them with food as they need it, He is certain to take care of His children!

But if we give up worrying, what will we do with all the time we spent being anxious? Exchange it for time in prayer. Go before God with your concerns. Cast all your cares on Him, for He promises to care for you. Tell God what you need, and thank Him in advance for what He will do. God will always provide. He will always show up. He does not want you to worry.

Lord, replace my worry time with prayer time. It is in Jesus'
name that I come before You now, presenting You with my
requests. Thank You for Your provision in my life. Amen.

Spiritual Eyes

"Do not be afraid, for those who are with us are more than those who are with them." Then Elisha prayed and said, "O Lord, please open his eyes that he may see." So the Lord opened the eyes of the young man, and he saw, and behold, the mountain was full of horses and chariots of fire all around Elisha.
2 Kings 6:16–17 esv

Some days, it seems like trouble follows us wherever we go, even though we are following the Lord of lords. Yet, we need not ever be shaken or alarmed when the trouble against us seems not only swift but also overwhelming. We need not be like Elisha's servant, who rose early one morning, went outside, saw the Syrian army with its horses and chariots surrounding the city, and panicked, asking his master what they should do.

Instead, may we remember that as God's children, we need not be afraid of anything in this world. For although at times unseen, God has more of His agents surrounding us, shielding us, than any earthly enemy. All we need to do is open the spiritual eyes of our faith to see the truth of the matter.

Lord God, You who are my sun and shield, when trouble comes my way, remind me to open my spiritual eyes and see Your agents surrounding me, a force bigger, stronger, and more powerful than any other that may seek my harm. Amen.

An Ever-Flowing Spring

"The LORD will guide you continually, giving you water when you are dry and restoring your strength. You will be like a well-watered garden, like an ever-flowing spring."

ISAIAH 58:11 NLT

It's easy to fall into the trap of looking to earthly things to restore us. Instead of immediately looking to the one who made us and knows every detail of what we need, we often look other places. The Lord is our water when we are dry. He restores our strength. As we look to Him, we will become like a lush, well-watered garden. Fruitful. Energetic. Growing.

This is one of those verses to keep close to your heart during a busy season. When it feels like your next day of rest is far off, this is a promise to cling to and draw strength from. Every day, as often as you can, make space for quiet moments with the Lord. A few moments can give you everything you need. Even as you fall asleep at night, this passage can be one you recite to bring you into a peaceful rest.

The Lord will restore you as you choose to take time to meditate on His Word and sit in His presence. When you are seeking out the right source, you will find you can make it through even the most rigorous of weeks.

My eyes are set on You, and You restore me.
As a gentle rain brings life to the driest soil, so Your
very presence and love bring life to my soul.

Unceasing Wonders

Many, LORD my God, are the wonders you have done, the things you planned for us. None can compare with you; were I to speak and tell of your deeds, they would be too many to declare.

PSALM 40:5 NIV

Think about all the amazing people you know and the wonderful impact they've had on the world. Certainly, you know women who have selflessly cared for the sick and dying. You probably know a handful of men and women who have donated thousands of dollars to charity. Perhaps you're acquainted with someone who's invention has improved the world. All are fantastic contributions, for sure. But when you think of the wonders of God, can anything really compare?

The honest answer is no—because there is no end to His wonders. Creation. Miracles. Salvation. Blessings. His love. His grace. His glory. His omnipotence. His omniscience. His power. His compassion. It's not even possible to name them all because His wonders continue even now! But sadly, our human tendency is to *ooh* and *aah* over the accomplishments and generosity of men and women while often overlooking the limitless love and power of our heavenly Father.

Take a moment right now to increase your joy by thinking on the wonders of our God. And then, spend time in quiet conversation with the one who loves you most.

God of unceasing wonders, forgive me for all the times I've failed to recognize Your greatness. Nothing compares to You!

Deep in Our Hearts

For this God is our God for ever and ever;
he will be our guide even to the end.
PSALM 48:14 NIV

You turn a corner on a busy street and, suddenly, you don't know where you are. You don't recognize the signs, the buildings, or the landmarks. You go back the way you came. You pause to think, to focus, trying not to panic. But it's no good. You know in your heart that you're off course and won't be able to find your way back without help.

And so it goes with our souls. We take many of the wrong paths in life. Then we backtrack. Then we take the wrong roads all over again. And again. Oh dear. We get scared, but we still want to go it alone. Or perhaps we reach out to the wrong people for help.

Still we search.

Deep in our hearts we know the truth, even if we spend a lifetime trying to deny it.

We're horribly lost.

We need someone to rescue us. We need the one who can take us by the heart and hand and give us a way out of our peril. Give us new life. And take us home where we belong.

There is only one who can be called on for that kind of mighty and supernatural rescue.

His name is Jesus.

Take heart. Your rescuer is here.

Lord, please set me free from sin and sadness. Let me walk on higher
ground with You by my side, for now and all eternity. Amen.

Benefits and Blessings

Bless (affectionately, gratefully praise) the Lord, O my
soul; and all that is [deepest] within me, bless His holy
name! Bless (affectionately, gratefully praise) the Lord,
O my soul, and forget not [one of] all His benefits.
PSALM 103:1–2 AMPC

When you're having a rough day, when your faith needs a boost, when you need to get your head in a better place, remember all the good things with which God blesses you.

God not only forgives but forgets all your misdeeds; and He heals all your maladies. He pulls you up from the pit of corruption and crowns you with not just favor but compassion. He fills your life with goodness and renews your youth like the eagles'. God brings justice to those who are treated unfairly and reveals Himself and His power.

Then, He really hits the heartstrings by being so full of mercy and grace toward you, slow in becoming angry, and filled with plenty of love and kindness. He won't stay angry nor hold a grudge. But the most amazing part of all this is that your Abba, your Father, doesn't punish you for all your sins, not as you deserve. Why? Because your God is all about love, which is more vast than you can imagine and which will never fail.

Today, count all those benefits. Then tonight, fall asleep counting all your blessings.

Lord, You overwhelm me with Your love—and so
much more. Let me count Your many blessings.

Finding Joy

And now, dear brothers and sisters, one final thing. Fix your thoughts on what is true, and honorable, and right, and pure, and lovely, and admirable. Think about things that are excellent and worthy of praise. Keep putting into practice all you learned and received from me—everything you heard from me and saw me doing. Then the God of peace will be with you.
PHILIPPIANS 4:8–9 NLT

Your mind is powerful. The thoughts you choose to dwell on have the power to determine the outcome of your day. They can pave the way for a calm and grateful heart or set a course for cynicism and disbelief.

There is such a benefit to fixing your thoughts on things that are good, pleasing, and perfect. God was not being legalistic when He said to think on these things. He was giving us sound advice. He was showing us the path to peace. What makes your heart beat a little faster? What brings joy to your heart and a smile to your lips? What makes your eyes crinkle with laughter and your feet step a little lighter? Think about these things.

Life is meant to be enjoyed. Relish the simple things! God made the playful puppies, galloping horses, and singing birds. He enjoys them, and He invites you to enjoy them too.

Oh Lord, You delight in every detail of my life! Surely that includes every wonderful moment and every bubble of laughter. May I fully indulge in the joy of life today.

The Secret Place

*He who dwells in the secret place of the Most High shall
remain stable and fixed under the shadow of the Almighty
[Whose power no foe can withstand]. I will say of the
Lord, He is my Refuge and my Fortress, my God; on Him
I lean and rely, and in Him I [confidently] trust!*
PSALM 91:1–2 AMPC

What benefits are available to the woman who dwells in that "secret place" of God—"whose power no foe can withstand"—making Him her absolute refuge and fortress!

For once she makes God her dwelling and confidently trusts Him, she'll be delivered from every danger. She knows she can run under His wings and find shelter. Her shield shall be His truth. She'll fear no terrors, knowing they can never reach her. She cannot be destroyed, so disease and death don't scare her.

Find your way into that secret place where you'll find a calmness of heart and focus of mind. Constantly remind yourself there's no power greater than that of the Almighty. Trust that you can remain there always, that He is available to you 24/7, no matter where you are. Make the words of Psalm 91:1–2 your mantra. And reap the benefits—in heaven and on earth.

*I'm looking to You for refuge, Lord. Beam me up to that
secret place. Help me to remain in You—no matter
what's going on in my life. In You alone I trust.*

The Gift of Peace

"Peace I leave with you; my peace I give you. I do not give to you as the world gives. Do not let your hearts be troubled and do not be afraid."

JOHN 14:27 NIV

Watching the news every day is enough to make anyone uneasy and restless, especially if the news stories are happening nearby. People disappear every day, children are abused, and cities are torn apart by rioting and looting. There seems to be no end to the evil that abounds in every city and town across our country. How can anyone live in peace under those circumstances?

As Christians, we can have peace even in the face of all the tragedy happening around us. Jesus made a promise to His disciples and to us as well. He was going back to the Father, but He was giving us a priceless gift. He gave us His peace. The world can never give us the peace that Jesus gives. It's a peace that we, the recipients, can't even understand. It's too wonderful for our minds to grasp, but we know it comes from Him.

Whatever is happening in your world, Christ can give you peace. None of the problems you're facing are too big for Him, whether it's trouble in the city where you live or pain in your own home. He is saying to you, don't let your heart be troubled about these things, and don't be afraid.

*Jesus, I ask for Your peace to fill my heart and mind.
Help me not to be afraid of the problems I'm facing.*

Can't You Hear Him Whisper?

He says, "Be still, and know that I am God."
PSALM 46:10 NIV

Our society is so fast-paced there is little time to take care of our mental and physical health, let alone our spiritual health. We are beings created for eternity, and we are made in the image of a supernatural God, and yet paying attention to our spiritual journey gets put off and off and off.

Until something terrible happens. Like a financial crisis. Or infidelity in our marriage. Or bad news at the doctor's office. Or a death in the family. Then, we do far more than pause. We go into a full-body panic mode, drenched in fear, racing around, grasping at anything and everything, desperate for answers. For peace.

But had we been in close fellowship with the Lord all along, we wouldn't be so frantic, our spirits so riddled with terror. What we need to do is to be still and know that He is God. Know that He is still in control, even though we think the bad news is in control. It's not. God is.

Life would be more peaceful, more focused, more infused with joy if we were already in the midst of communion with God when troubles come.

Can't you hear Him whisper to you, "Be still, and know that I am God"?

*Lord, help me to want to spend time with You every day
of my life—in fair weather as well as stormy. Amen.*

In His Hands

*Jesus answered them, "Do you finally believe? In fact,
you're about to make a run for it—saving your own skins and
abandoning me. But. . .the Father is with me. I've told you all
this so that. . .you will be unshakable and assured, deeply at
peace. In this godless world you will continue to experience
difficulties. But take heart! I've conquered the world."*
JOHN 16:33 MSG

As Christ-followers, it's easy to become discouraged in a world that seems to move further and further away from Jesus. The gap becomes more pronounced by the day. Wars. Disease. Natural disasters. Political unrest. It seems there's one crisis after another. And even those who follow Christ could be pulled into the fray if our focus is too much on the world and not enough on Jesus. Our anxiety and depression may threaten to spiral out of control. We may even lose hope.

But. . .just as God didn't abandon His Son on the cross, Jesus assured His disciples that He was still in control and always would be—because He conquered the world! So, take heart, dear one. As bad as things might seem, our heavenly Father has us in His hands—today, tomorrow, and for eternity! With the unfailing promise of Jesus, we have lasting joy, peace, comfort, and hope!

*Lord, because of Your unfailing promises, I always have
hope. As the world grows apart from You, draw me closer
to Your heart. Thank You for Your love and salvation!*

Celebrate Peace

Therefore, since we have been justified through faith,
we have peace with God through our Lord Jesus Christ.
ROMANS 5:1 NIV

The type of peace this verse is talking about isn't a feeling. It's the kind of peace that's like a peace treaty. When we ask Jesus to be Lord of our lives, our status and relationship with God change. We go from being His enemies to being His friends. Additionally, we have a sense of relief that His wrath and the punishment for our sins are no longer hanging over our heads.

We also can celebrate that peace with God is not just a onetime event. Rather, it is an ongoing source of blessing. Peace *with* God leads to peace *from* God. And this peace is not just the absence of turmoil and trouble but a real sense that God is in control. It's a small representation of heaven here on earth. His peace brings the confidence that He is working things out in our lives, even if we can't understand it all.

Satan would love to steal our peace. He can't change our relationship with God, but we can give Satan a foothold when we worry and ruminate and fuss over our circumstances instead of turning them over to God. Give your troubles to God and rest in His peace.

Dear God, as Your Son told us, we will have trouble in this
world. But You have overcome the world. Remind us to
rest in Your presence and in the knowledge that You are
working everything out according to a plan far beyond our
comprehension. Thank You for Your watchful love. Amen.

The Hand of God

*For I am the LORD your God who takes hold of your right
hand and says to you, Do not fear; I will help you.*
ISAIAH 41:13 NIV

If there is a scripture you need to have handy in times of trouble, this is it! Post it on your fridge; write it on a sticky note to tack up in your car; commit it to memory so that the Spirit of God can bring it to mind when you need to hear it most.

Psalm 139 tells us that God created us and knows everything about us. He knows when we sit and when we get up, and He knows every word that's on our tongue before we speak it. Psalm 139:7–10 tells us that no matter where we go, His hand will guide us and hold us.

Heading to the emergency room? Repeat Isaiah 41:13 and remember that God is holding your hand. Afraid of the future? Stop worrying and trust the God who loves you and has great plans for you. Facing a problem that you cannot possibly bear? Take hold of God's mighty hand and believe that He will help you.

*Father God, help me not to fear. Take hold of my hand and
guide me. I put my faith and trust in You alone. Amen.*

Let God Reign!

*Oh, how great are God's riches and wisdom and knowledge!
How impossible it is for us to understand his decisions and his
ways! For who can know the LORD's thoughts? Who knows enough
to give him advice? And who has given him so much that he needs
to pay it back? For everything comes from him and exists by his
power and is intended for his glory. All glory to him forever! Amen.*

ROMANS 11:33–36 NLT

It's easy for us to believe that we carry the world on our shoulders. We tend to think, though we may not admit it, that we alone make the world turn. We convince ourselves that worry, finances, or power will put us in control. But in truth, God is the one who controls all.

What a blessed peace awaits us! As you go about your day, rest in the assurance that God, not you, is in control. God understands every feeling you experience, and He can comfort you. God knows the best steps for you to take in life, and He is willing to guide you. He is above all and knows all, yet He is not out of reach.

Set your eyes firmly on the Lord, and He will care for you.

*Lord, please let this truth sink deep into my heart today
so that I may live in joy and peace. Please guide me by
Your wisdom and provide for me according to Your
riches. I praise You because You are good!*

The Ultimate Security

*"You will know at last that I, the LORD, am your Savior
and your Redeemer, the Mighty One of Israel."*
ISAIAH 60:16 NLT

Do you ever wonder what life would be like if we *knew* that the Lord was our Savior and Redeemer, the Mighty One of Israel? What would our lives look like if we believed this with every fiber of our being? Take a moment to think about that. How would your attitude about today change? This passage goes on to say, "I will make peace your leader and righteousness your ruler" (Isaiah 60:17 NLT).

It is a worthy goal to seek the Lord in everything we do, to get to know Him better with each passing day. What would our lives look like if we knew, really *knew*, that He alone is our Savior and Redeemer? A holy fear—a great respect for God—would not be far from us, for we would understand that even mountains tremble before Him. Worry would drain away as we understood that He is the one who provides for every one of our needs. Even in the face of death, if that was what the Lord willed, we would be at peace, for then we would be even closer to meeting Him face-to-face. We would move forward in every opportunity with confidence. We would battle with courage, knowing our ultimate security is in God.

*Lord, may I know at last that You are the Lord,
my Savior and Redeemer. You are the Mighty One
of Israel and forever my deepest desire.*

Antidote to Worry

*"So don't worry about tomorrow, for tomorrow will bring
its own worries. Today's trouble is enough for today."*
MATTHEW 6:34 NLT

It has been said that today is the tomorrow you worried about yesterday. Isn't it true? And how much of the things you worry about actually happen? Worry is a thief. It robs us of the joy of the moment and plants us firmly in the future, where we have absolutely no control. Instead of focusing on the problems that this day brings, we propel ourselves into an unknown tomorrow. In living this way, we miss out on all the little moments that make life precious.

The antidote to worry is to focus on today—this hour, this moment in time. What is happening now? Experience it with all five of your senses. Allow the wonder of today to touch your heart and settle it down. Sure, there is trouble today, and there are problems to solve, but Jesus is right here with us. We have the gift of the Holy Spirit who can counsel and comfort us and help us get through any and every situation. There is nothing you can't face with Jesus by your side. When you focus on what He can do instead of what you can't do, you will experience a deep and abiding peace that comes only from Him.

*Lord, worry is such a part of who I am! When I'm not worried,
I worry that I'm missing something. Please help me not to
worry about tomorrow. Help me to focus on today, on what is
happening now, and to let You take care of all my trouble. Amen.*

Our Forever Home

Lord, through all the generations you have been our home!
Before the mountains were born, before you gave birth to the
earth and the world, from beginning to end, you are God.
PSALM 90:1–2 NLT

Here, the psalmist is praising God. He is celebrating the consistent character of the heavenly Father, who does not change (Hebrews 13:8), who has been the "home" of humanity since the beginning of time, and who will continue to be our home for all eternity.

When you think of *home*, what comes to mind? What emotions do you feel? . . . Comfort, love, calm, family, warmth, acceptance, forgiveness, joy, fun. . . For some, there really is no place like home. But for others, home isn't warm and fuzzy—instead, it's been filled with hardship and strain, sadness and chaos.

No matter what your home is like right now—or has been like in the past—there is good news: we've all received an invitation to a *forever home* with Jesus. And home with Him offers everything our souls crave—peace, beauty, tranquility, grace, love without limits. . . It's the home we've always longed for, and the door is wide open, complete with a WELCOME mat outside. Take a step inside your forever home today.

Father God, I accept Your invitation to my forever home with
You. Thank You for being such a good Father, for giving me love
and grace, peace and comfort—all the things my soul craves!

A Good Word

Anxiety in the heart of man causes depression,
but a good word makes it glad.
PROVERBS 12:25 NKJV

As most of us know, anxiety and depression are two sides of the same coin. According to this verse, keeping anxiety in our hearts causes depression. We are anxious about what might happen and we become depressed about what didn't. Anxiety and depression create a vicious cycle, keeping us bound to the past and paralyzed about the future.

But this proverb reminds us that "a good word makes [the heart] glad." Where can you get a good word? Philippians 4:8 (NLT) tells us to "fix [our] thoughts on what is true, and honorable, and right, and pure, and lovely, and admirable. Think about things that are excellent and worthy of praise." This is a good word! We know it to be true experientially, and studies prove that reading the Bible, singing praise songs, and hearing encouraging words from friends can literally change our brain's chemistry and lift a dark mood. These good words replace the anxiety and depression in our hearts with joy and peace in the Holy Spirit.

Father, my heart is sometimes weighed down by anxiety. I know
what it feels like to be depressed. Thank You for Your Word and
the reminder that I don't have to settle for these feelings. Thank
You that I can trust You to bring joy back to my soul. Amen.

Cure for Discontent

Always giving thanks for all things in the name of
our Lord Jesus Christ to our God and Father.
EPHESIANS 5:20 NASB

Do you struggle with being satisfied with your current situation in life? Discontent is a heart disease that manifests in comparing, coveting, and complaining. What is the cure? The habit of gratitude. Thanking God for everything—the good and the bad—means we accept it as His will, even if we don't like it.

Sometimes, we receive birthday or Christmas gifts we have no desire for, but we still thank the giver. God is the good giver of every perfect gift (James 1:17). Failing to thank Him is rebellion against His wisdom and ways. If we expect Him to do things the way we want or to give us more, we forget that God owes us nothing.

When God commands thanksgiving, He is not mandating our feelings but rather our submission. However, because thankfulness changes our attitude and outlook, it does affect our feelings. Discontent and resentment cannot coexist with humble acceptance of what happens to us. Therefore, thanking God must become our lifelong habit. When we turn out the light every night, we can review our day and thank God for each event—good and bad—because He allowed it and He is good. We can be satisfied with that.

Bountiful Father, I'm sorry I often rebel against Your sovereign
plan for me. Thank You for doing all things well. Your essence
is love, and every mark You make in my life is a love mark,
conforming me to Christ. I accept Your will and Your ways.

From Chaos to Calm

And they came to Him and awoke Him, saying, "Master, Master, we are perishing!" Then He arose and rebuked the wind and the raging of the water. And they ceased, and there was a calm.

LUKE 8:24 NKJV

Our hearts go out to the disciples who faced the storm while traveling in a small boat upon the sea. How terrified they must've been as the small vessel tipped this way and that, thunder crashing overhead, rain pouring down on their heads, lightning streaking across the sky.

Jesus was never afraid of the storm. In fact, He was able to sleep through it, completely at peace. How we long to be like Him! How wonderful to trust Him so fully that we can be at rest even when storms rage around us. With just a word, our precious Savior can calm the storms in our lives. He speaks, and thunder seals its lips. He lifts His hand, and lightning tucks itself away behind a cloud. Even drops of rain cease at His command.

There'll be storms. But you can trust Jesus to stay in the boat with you, even when you're tipping to and fro. He'll never leave you. He's right there, whispering, "Peace, be still!"

Lord, so many times I've found myself in the proverbial raging seas, and it's exhausting. Fear overwhelms me. Thank You for the reminder that a simple word, a whisper from You, and storms in my life cease. Speak now, Father, I pray. Amen.

Thank God

Hallelujah! Thank GOD! And why? Because he's good, because his love lasts. But who on earth can do it—declaim GOD's mighty acts, broadcast all his praises? You're one happy man when you do what's right, one happy woman when you form the habit of justice.
PSALM 106:1–3 MSG

Are you in the habit of thanking God? Taking one minute each morning to turn your thoughts toward thanks to God can change the outlook of your entire day. Maybe you woke up to the reminder of all the extra work on your plate this week. Maybe your children didn't sleep well last night but you have a nonstop day today. Maybe you just don't feel like being in a good mood!

Stop. Just stop what you're thinking for a moment and focus your mind on God. Allow His Spirit inside you to remind you of His goodness. His love lasts. Always. Now thank Him for at least one great blessing in your life right now.

You are the only one in charge of your attitude. Many things will happen today—some good, some maybe not so good—but all are outside of your control. You can control how you respond to everything that happens this day. Why not thank God no matter what? Think that might change how well your day goes? Why not give it a try and see what happens!

God, please remind me in this moment of Your goodness and Your great love for me! Please help me to choose You in each moment. Help me thank You in every circumstance. Amen.

Celebrate!

It is a good and delightful thing to give thanks to the Lord, to sing praises. . .to Your name, O Most High, to show forth Your loving-kindness in the morning and Your faithfulness by night. . . . For You, O Lord, have made me glad by Your works; at the deeds of Your hands I joyfully sing.
PSALM 92:1–2, 4 AMPC

Some people record their blessings. They keep a journal where they write down the good things that happen every day. This helps them maintain a positive outlook on life and serves as a great reminder that the bad days really aren't *all* bad. There is good in every bad day too!

Here in Psalm 92, something good has happened, and the psalmist is celebrating and showing his delight in song: "You, O Lord, have made me glad by Your works; at the deeds of Your hands I joyfully sing." Journaling your blessings or singing about them—either way, both are wonderful expressions of the heavenly Father's goodness in everyday living.

This world, while often difficult, doesn't have to leave us down and depressed. When we belong to Jesus, we have the promise of His blessing. We have the benefit of His kindness and goodness. And if we keep our focus on those things, our emotional wellness will benefit mightily. Praise Him!

God, You are so, so good. Help me to keep my focus on Your loving-kindness. Thank You for these wonderful things that happened today.

Difficult Weeks

The Lord hears his people when they call to him
for help. He rescues them from all their troubles.
PSALM 34:17 NLT

We all go through difficult seasons. Sometimes, they stretch over many days, filling up a whole week. Health challenges. Financial woes. Relationship struggles. They can be so frustrating and interrupt the daily flow of things. Nothing seems—or feels—right.

Today, as you think about the rough weeks you've faced in your life, pause for a moment to remember the week before Jesus' crucifixion. He rode into Jerusalem with "Hosannas!" ringing out all around Him, but things took a turn for the worse pretty quickly. In just a matter of days, He went from "local hero" to persecuted, beaten, bruised, betrayed, and crucified.

We could stop right there and be filled with a sense of desperation, but thank goodness, the story goes on. A new week began the following Sunday—a week of resurrection and glory as Jesus came forth from the grave! In much the same way, our bad seasons will turn around. New life will come. Hope will be restored. The key lies in not giving up. Trust Him. Even when it doesn't make sense. The grave clothes are coming off! He's breathing new life into your family, your situations, your finances, and your very soul.

Father, I know You understand! What a terrible week Your Son faced
in Jerusalem. I can't even imagine all He went through, but it must
have broken Your heart. Thank You for the reminder that the next
week was filled with resurrection power! This brings me such hope!

Love and Assurance

*Little children, let's not love with word or with tongue, but in deed
and truth. We will know by this that we are of the truth, and will
set our heart at ease before Him, that if our heart condemns us
that God is greater than our heart, and He knows all things.*

1 JOHN 3:18–20 NASB

These verses start out with an admonition: you ought to show your love
in what you do. Love is not well expressed by superficial, noncommittal
statements. Rather, a true, earnest love will drive you to action. Think
about those around you to whom you can express love, not just by telling
them but by showing your love to them in your deeds. Don't allow laziness
or excuses to keep you from reaching out to those who need love.

These verses end with a wonderful assurance for those of us who
struggle with guilt and fear. When you are in Christ, be encouraged that
nothing can take away your salvation. Your heart may condemn you when
you fall into the same pattern of sin again or when you fail to do what you
promised yourself and God you would do. But be encouraged—you are
not in charge of your standing before God. God is. He is greater than any
guilt-ridden and self-abasing heart. Once you are one of His children, you
will always have that status. He knows all things, including the fact that
your name is written, irrevocably, in the book of life.

*Lord, help me to show love not only in what I say,
but even more so in what I do. Thank You that You
are greater than the fears of my heart.*

Perfection

*For I am confident of this very thing, that He
who began a good work among you will
complete it by the day of Christ Jesus.*

<small>PHILIPPIANS 1:6 NASB</small>

The Lord is working in you—you are a work in progress! He has started a good work in you that has not yet been completed. Take this truth to heart and don't be overly discouraged when you fall into the same sin patterns—God is working in you. If you ever feel that you must not be saved because you're struggling with things that you shouldn't struggle with as a Christian, be encouraged that no matter how it feels to you, from the moment you were saved God started working in you. On the days when it doesn't feel like God is working at all, remind yourself of Philippians 1:6.

God will perfect the work He has started in you. Even if there are road bumps along the way, He *will* complete and perfect His work in you. He won't abandon you if you don't perform up to some standard. He perfects the good work in you because He desires that you be more like Him and that you walk in closer relationship with Him. So be encouraged and try to recognize the areas in which God has already been perfecting His work in your life. You are on a good and perfect trajectory.

*Lord, thank You that You are working in me even when
I don't feel it. Thank You that You will not abandon the
work that You have started in me, no matter what.*

Dwelling on the Important Things

Set your mind on things above, not on things on the earth.
COLOSSIANS 3:2 NKJV

Andrea spent the morning cooking and baking, getting ready for a family get-together at her sister's house. She worked hard on each of her dishes, especially the pie, then loaded the food into the car and drove to her sister's. Delicious food covered the kitchen counter, and Andrea added her contributions to the bounty. When it came time for dessert, Andrea sliced into the pie she had spent time carefully putting together. To her dismay, the filling had not set like it should have. Disappointment clouded her day. In spite of the good time she had visiting with everyone, she felt her time and money had been wasted on the pie.

Sometimes, we worry about little things and forget to look at the big picture. If all we see are the things that go wrong or the trouble around us, we have missed what's important. Instead of focusing on spending time with her family, Andrea fretted about how long it had taken her to fix the pie and how much money she had spent on the ingredients.

As Christians, we can focus on our problems and the little things that frustrate us, or we can keep our minds on heavenly things and know we have hope beyond what troubles us here. Christ is bigger than anything we may have to endure here on earth.

Lord, help us to keep our minds fixed on You so that the problems we face are seen through Your grace in our lives.

Peace-Bringer

For God is not a God of disorder but of peace.
1 Corinthians 14:33 niv

Orderliness in life brings peace, whereas disorderliness leads to confusion and chaos. This is a simple truth from God. Like warm, clean, colorful laundry tossed together, the moments and activities of our day need sorting into harmony. Balance rest with work, reflection with business, and togetherness with solitude. Determine ways to let your day and week reflect the orderliness of God.

Because you are made in God's image, you have a great capacity to bring tranquility from disorder in your home. Does your home feel tranquil? If not, consider giving away extra items.

Along with *not* being a God of disorder, God is also *not* a God of confusion. So take time to consider your emotions and thoughts. Sort through them and ask the Holy Spirit to guide you into peace. Your inner world of thoughts and feelings thrive when you slow down for reflection. Is there something that needs to be said? Is there a trouble that needs to be given to God in prayer? You can be certain Jesus, your Prince of Peace, will lead you from confusion to calm if you will only ask Him.

God, You know the struggles both inside and outside of me. Please come into this chaos and bring Your peace. I choose You to be the center of my day and my life instead of the confusion that abounds without You.

More Than Sparrows

"You are worth more than many sparrows."
Matthew 10:31 niv

Sparrows are not rare birds. The little gray, white, and black bodies can be spotted all over the world. They hang out in hedges and graze on grassland. They are about as common as field mice and bunny rabbits.

But as common as they are, God knows these creatures. He knows the seeds they like to eat and when they molt. He knows they like to bathe in the dust and congregate in talkative groups. He knows the feathers on their heads and the bird's-eye views they have seen.

God cares about sparrows. He cares about caterpillars and ants and bunny rabbits and (shudder!) mice as well. And if our great God cares about these little creatures that come and go and do as they please, how much more do you think He cares about you? Even when you're struggling to follow Him and when you sing the wrong notes in all the right praise songs and when you forget to pray and when you forget you know Him—in all these times, the God of the sparrows and the grass in the field and the mountaintops and the nations knows you and claims you as His child.

Do not ever worry about what you are worth to your Father. He loves you more than the wildflowers growing in the field. He loves you more than the flutter of a million sparrows' wings. He sees you and everything you do from His God's-eye view, and He loves you still.

God, thank You for making me feel precious. Amen.

Peace beyond Comprehension

*Do not be anxious about anything, but in every situation,
by prayer and petition, with thanksgiving, present your requests
to God. And the peace of God, which transcends all understanding,
will guard your hearts and your minds in Christ Jesus.*
PHILIPPIANS 4:6–7 NIV

Within the first hours of the day, many of us can find opportunities to worry. But as we learn to take every situation to God, He exchanges our worries for His peace.

We come before God and bring Him our needs, knowing He is the only one who can grant our request. And we are to do this with thanksgiving. When we remember all God has done for us and provided for us, the worries that cause us to focus on what we don't have slip away in the presence of our mighty God.

God has compassion on us and knows we have many things we worry about. He tells us many times to come to Him. In 1 Peter 5:7, He tells us to give Him our cares. In Matthew 6:25, He tells us He will provide for us and meet our needs.

God promises that peace will permeate both our hearts, where our feelings can churn painfully, and our minds, where we can turn situations over endlessly. Along with giving us His peace, God takes our minds into protective custody, cutting off worries before they can enter.

*Lord Jesus, thank You for giving us Your supernatural
peace. Remind us to bring all of our cares to You and
to thank You for everything You've done for us.*

Choosing Faith

Be still in the presence of the LORD, and wait patiently for him to act. Don't worry about evil people who prosper or fret about their wicked schemes. Stop being angry! Turn from your rage! Do not lose your temper—it only leads to harm. For the wicked will be destroyed, but those who trust in the LORD will possess the land.

PSALM 37:7–9 NLT

Our faith is tested when life doesn't go the way we expect it to, when people who aren't following God prosper and we seem to be an afterthought. At times, we even go so far as to blame God for the things that are going wrong.

Even though it seems like the wicked are prospering and we are not, our daily grind is not in vain. Each day we are faithful is another seed planted. It may take time for it to grow, but grow it will. There will be a harvest.

Faith sees the facts but trusts God anyway. Faith is forcing yourself to worry no longer but to pray in earnest and leave the situation in His hands. Faith is choosing to trust and rest in His plan rather than fret about what could happen. We must choose faith even when we don't feel it. It is through choosing faith that we please God. Choose faith, and see what He will do.

Lord, despite what logic or the world tells me, I choose now to let my worries go and have faith in You. I trust that You will take care of every need, and I lay down all my burdens at Your feet.

Your Best Life

Keep my words and store up my commands. . . . Keep my commands and you will live; guard my teachings as the apple of your eye. Bind them on your fingers; write them on the tablet of your heart. Say to wisdom, "You are my sister," and to insight, "You are my relative."

PROVERBS 7:1–4 NIV

Keep. Store up. Guard. Bind. Write. Say. Do *all* these things with God's Word, and you will have life—*your best life*, that is. Because God's Word *is* life, and we were created to live by it. When we become intimately familiar with biblical truth, then we have a strong foundation for a truly wonderful life.

When hard times come—*and they will*—a knowledge of God's hope and healing will bring you through.

When temptations come—*and they will*—God's teachings will help you stay on the path of faith and truth.

When enemies attack—*and they will*—God's promise of protection and victory will shelter you.

What are you struggling with today, beautiful soul? Whatever it is, trust God and His Word to carry you through it. His Words will bring you strength, comfort, and peace of mind. Open your Bible and see what He has to say. Meditate on the message God has just for you.

Keep. Store up. Guard. Bind. Write. Say. Repeat!

God, You are all good things. Help me to live my best life with You and Your Word front and center!

He Is with You

"Do not fear, for I am with you; do not be afraid, for I am your God. I will strengthen you, I will also help you, I will also uphold you with My righteous right hand."

ISAIAH 41:10 NASB

Fear can seep into our lives so easily. We fear the unknowns of the future. We fear we didn't handle a certain situation as well as we should have. We fear we are too inadequate or too busy or too unmotivated to handle the things being thrown at us in the present.

But in this verse, God tells you not to fear. This isn't just an idle, "don't worry, you'll be okay" kind of statement. In fact, He *commands* you not to fear. How can He be so confident that you are completely safe so that He can command you not to fear? Because He is with you. The God who created, sustains, and governs this entire world is with you. With that perspective, what is there to fear?

Stop looking anxiously around you at all the burdens, worries, and fears of your life. Instead, focus on your God. He promises to strengthen and help you. Nothing in this world is so overwhelming that you cannot overcome it with the almighty God's strength. And even when you feel that you have fallen with no strength to get up, He promises to hold you up with His hand.

Lord, help me to fully understand that You are with me, strengthening me, helping me, and holding me in Your hands.

Trust and Lean

*Trust in the LORD with all your heart and do
not lean on your own understanding.*

PROVERBS 3:5 NASB

This verse contains two commands—trust in the Lord and don't rely on your own understanding.

Do you trust in God? You can rely on God because He is truly trustworthy—He has the strength to sustain, help, and protect you and an incomprehensible love for you that cannot be broken or grow stale. You are not bringing your prayers before someone who is powerful but fickle, or one who is loving and good, but weak. You pray to a God who is all-powerful, but also good and loving. Therefore, you can be confident that your life is placed firmly in His hands and His control and that He considers it precious.

How often do you lean on your own understanding and strength instead of God's? You are remarkably less capable of controlling your life than God is. Instead of trusting yourself, someone who doesn't know the future and certainly can't control it, lean on the all-powerful God who knows each step you will take. Relinquish all your anxious thoughts over to His control. Trusting God with your future is far more productive than worrying about it. So lean on Him and trust Him with *everything* in your heart. He will sustain you.

*Lord, forgive me for not trusting You as I should. Forgive
me for leaning on my own understanding instead of relying
on Your infinite wisdom and strength. Thank You that these
commands You give me are for my greatest benefit.*

The Right Focus

Turning your ear to wisdom and applying your heart to understanding—indeed, if you call out for insight and cry aloud for understanding, and if you look for it as for silver and search for it as for hidden treasure, then you will understand the fear of the LORD and find the knowledge of God.
PROVERBS 2:2–5 NIV

If you've ever lost something—your keys, your glasses, or an important document—you've no doubt searched everywhere. Sometimes when you finally find it, you realize that in your haste, you simply overlooked the very thing you were frantically searching for.

It's all about focus! Even when you're looking in the right direction, you can still miss something because your focus is slightly off. This can be the challenge in our relationship with God. We can ask God a question and be really intent on getting the answer, only to find that His response to us was there all along—just not the answer we expected or wanted.

Frustration and stress can keep us from clearly seeing the things that God puts before us. Time spent in prayer and meditation on God's Word can often wash away the dirt and grime of the day-to-day and provide a clear picture of God's intentions for our lives. Step outside the pressure and into His presence, and get the right focus for whatever you're facing today.

Lord, help me to avoid distractions and keep my eyes on You. Amen.

Dust

Just as a father has compassion on his children, so the LORD has compassion on those who fear Him. For He Himself knows our frame; He is mindful that we are nothing but dust.
PSALM 103:13–14 NASB

Do you ever feel weak or inconsequential? Or like the slightest wind of difficulty could just blow you away? These verses tell you that you are but dust and that God is aware of that. That doesn't sound very encouraging, does it? But when you think about it, great strength can be gleaned from this truth.

The Lord knows your frame. He knows that at times you are prone to weakness and worry and lack the strength to continue. So if you are harboring guilt that you have not lived up to some heavenly standard that you feel God has placed on you, release that guilt. He is mindful of what you are capable of and doesn't ask that you be some kind of superwoman. This is not an excuse for complacency or laziness but an encouragement that your efforts are recognized and smiled on by God.

Even though you are but a speck of dust in the history of the universe, God has compassion on you and knows you as a father knows his child. How stunning! It doesn't matter that you sometimes feel weak and inconsequential—the Most High God knows and loves you. In that truth resides all the strength and value you need.

Lord, thank You that You know my frame. Please grant me the strength and value that I long for.

Bloom and Grow

"Their lives will be like a well-watered garden, never again left to dry up. Young women will dance and be happy, young men and old men will join in. I'll convert their weeping into laughter."

JEREMIAH 31:12–13 MSG

Imagine a dead, withered flower garden. Brown leaves rustle and scatter in the breeze; full, colorful blooms have faded; a once-lovely floral aroma has been overtaken by the smell of death and decay. This sad, lifeless flower garden bears resemblance to our lives without Christ. Without Him, we have no sunshine, no rain, no pruning—no life! When He's missing, our story is devoid of hope and light.

But *with* Him? . . . When Christ is front and center in our lives, we are like a well-cared-for garden. Lush and bursting with color. . .an aroma, sweet and pleasant! We get just enough sunshine, the perfect amount of rain (right down to the last drop!). Our petals stretch out, colorful and full. And Christ continues to work, day by day, pruning and caring for us so that we can bloom and grow into the splendid daughters He meant for us to be.

On days when you feel dried up and hopeless, reach out to the master gardener. Allow Him to pluck, prune, and drench your parched soul in His love and compassion. He will bring what's dead to life again.

Master gardener, I invite You to work on the dried-up parts of my soul. Please give me light, hope, and life!

A No-Regrets Life

By the mercies of God. . .present your bodies as a living and holy sacrifice, acceptable to God, which is your spiritual service of worship. And do not be conformed to this world, but be transformed by the renewing of your mind, so that you may prove what the will of God is, that which is good and acceptable and perfect.

ROMANS 12:1–2 NASB

Regrettably, no one gets through life without regrets. Some nag us occasionally; others confront us daily. Even Jesus had regrets, not from His own decisions but from the unbelief and attacks of the people around Him. He responded with weeping at times and by saying, "Father, forgive them."

Often, we likewise regret how others have hurt us. And we deal with relationship conflicts, accidents, age and health issues, crime and corruption, along with burdens others impose on us. For situations beyond our control, Romans 12:1–2 offers the best way of handling hurts and regrets. Based on God's mercy, we can offer our lives and circumstances as a sacrifice to Him. We may struggle in doing this, but trusting God is the only safe option. Saying, "Your will be done," is a worshipful response that can become our mind-set for facing all of life's difficulties. We also need God's Word transforming our thinking. A renewed mind prevents us from conforming to the world's philosophies and temptations.

What will result? We will discover that God's will is good and acceptable and perfect for us. Knowing this truth nullifies regrets.

Merciful God, thank You for accepting what I offer up to You. Please take me—body, mind, and will. I surrender all.

Dependent on Him

*It is not that we think we are qualified to do anything
on our own. Our qualification comes from God.*

2 CORINTHIANS 3:5 NLT

You are in a hurry, and your patience begins to evaporate with each breath you take. Your preschooler is taking forever to get ready and now sits down on the floor, pulling his left shoe toward him.

Exasperated, you say for the second time, "Please, let Mommy help you with your shoes." But, of course, he wants to do it himself and works on it at a snail's pace. After what feels like hours, you make it into the car, drop him off at preschool, and head to work.

When you finally reach your destination, you suddenly realize as you pull into the parking lot that you often treat God like your child treated you that morning. You begin to imagine how God feels when *you* try to do things on your own.

This is the moment to breathe deeply and bow your head in prayer, inviting God to help you to depend more on Him—He who is your strength and your defense (see Isaiah 12:2), your protector, and your rescuer, He who is merely a breath away (see Psalm 145:18–20).

*Father, I know You stand ready to help me with whatever
task is at hand. I don't want to do it in my own ability but,
instead, surrender completely to do things Your way.*

Simply Shadows

So don't put up with anyone pressuring you in details of diet, worship services, or holy days. All those things are mere shadows cast before what was to come; the substance is Christ.
COLOSSIANS 2:16–17 MSG

Small things cast large shadows. If you have ever been frightened by something insignificant, you know this is true. In the same way, rigid man-made rules are little things that cast large shadows, ones that would steal your sunlight and joy. But Christ is your beautiful reality.

Christ is the solid substance of life. He is your sure footing and your rock. He doesn't change or falter. When you keep your eyes directed at Him and not the shadows, you focus on what is real. Allowing His truth to seep in deeply will allow your mind to be "confident and at rest" (Colossians 2:2–4 MSG).

Looking at the real thing, knowing and being in touch with who Christ really is, helps you pick out what's false, enabling you to eliminate it from your life. So pay no attention to the worldly rules of others, their hollow philosophies, human traditions—"men's ideas of the material rather than the spiritual world" (Colossians 2:8 AMPC)—that have no basis in God or His Word. Instead, live, breathe, and abide in Christ. *He* is your reality. He will keep you out of the shadows and lead you into His Sonlight!

There's no one like You, God! Help me to keep my eyes focused on You. Amen.

God's Gift: Power, Love, and a Sound Mind

*For God has not given us a spirit of fear, but of
power and of love and of a sound mind.*
2 TIMOTHY 1:7 NKJV

Have you ever been completely surprised and delighted by a present? God the Father has given each believer the amazing gift of His Spirit. This gift is too immense to wrap yet lives inside you so that you are never without it.

God has gifted you a spirit of *power*, for He knows you will have many battles to fight. You will need to endure hard times. You may need to defend yourself against those who would want you to think you are less than you are. Using your spirit of power for good will only confirm your courage.

God has given you a spirit of *love*. This gift whispers of endurance, grace, and even boldness. To love boldly despite past hurts isn't easy. But God's love triumphs over all obstacles. So don't be afraid to love others and yourself with abandonment.

A *sound mind* is a gift that is well balanced and keeps all things in calm perspective. When the chaos of the day begins to swirl around you, breathe deeply and remember you have the sound mind of Christ. It's steady and able to accurately prioritize the steps needed to flourish.

*Father God, I'm in awe of Your Spirit within me.
Thank You for Your amazing gift! Let power, love,
and a sound mind be my watchwords every day.*

Stop, Look, and Listen

"Work six days. The seventh day is a Sabbath, a day of
total and complete rest, a sacred assembly. Don't do any
work. Wherever you live, it is a Sabbath to GOD."
LEVITICUS 23:3 MSG

You may be one of those women for whom nothing is more satisfying than checking things off a to-do list. Groceries, check. Dinner plans, check. Kids' homework, check. Lunches packed, check. Project deadline met, check. Date night, check. Bible reading, check. Prayer, check.

Yet, amid this breakneck pace, you may be losing sight of something that is very important to God: a day of no to-dos. A day when you take a respite from the hectic. A day when you gather with those of like mind to stop, look, and listen to what God would have you be, see, and hear. A day to get in touch with your spiritual root—the vine, Christ—who on at least one occasion told His stressed-out disciples, "'Come off by yourselves; let's take a break and get a little rest.' For there was constant coming and going. They didn't even have time to eat" (Mark 6:31 MSG).

So stop. Take a day to sit and sup in Christ. Look for what the Holy Spirit is ready to teach you. Listen to what God has to say.

Here I am, Lord. Quiet. Still. Sitting before You.
Be with me. Reveal Yourself to me. Speak to
me as I melt into Your presence. Amen.

Healthy Heart

Pay attention to what I say; turn your ear to my words. Do not let them out of your sight, keep them within your heart; for they are life to those who find them and health to one's whole body.

PROVERBS 4:20–22 NIV

How's your heart health? The health of your heart, the source of all your emotions, is critical to the well-being of your entire body. Unfortunately, there can be toxic waste accumulations within your heart that need to be brought to light and replaced with brilliant truth.

God commands you to put His truths into your heart by meditating on His Word. Truths transform your thoughts. Truths toss out lies you have believed about yourself. You live in a broken world; therefore, your mind requires a heavenly wipe down, a renewal that transforms you. After reading this devotion, take a few words from a verse that means something to you and turn them over all day in your mind.

God stresses the importance of guarding well your heart where His truths are stored, truths that bring you life and healing. When you hear the voice in your head—the one that says you are a failure, stupid, too much or not enough—raise your shield and grab your sword. Meditate on what God says about you. You are holy, without blame, more than a conqueror, a beloved child of God, alive in Christ.

God, help me replace my earthly thoughts
with Your heavenly truths. Amen.

Alone with God

*God is our refuge and strength, always ready to
help in times of trouble. So we will not fear.*
PSALM 46:1–2 NLT

At times, you may hear about war or see devastation wrought by earthquakes, fires, hurricanes, famine, tornadoes, and tsunamis. There is only one place you can go to escape all the chaos.

God is your refuge, high tower, fortress, stronghold, strength. He is there at the first sign of trouble in every area of your life—within and without. He is your go-to God.

He commands you: "Be still, and know that I am God!" (Psalm 46:10 NLT). He will diminish your fears, realign your thoughts with His, settle an overwhelming peace on you, and give you a new vision.

A blind man was brought to Jesus. He took him by the hand, away from the crowd. After His first touch, the blind man saw people but they looked like trees walking. Then, when Jesus touched his eyes again, the man's sight was fully restored. "He could see everything clearly" (Mark 8:25 NLT).

Allow God to lead you away to a place where you and He can be alone. Allow Him to give you new sight and knowledge in the stillness of His presence.

*Here I am, Lord. Still before You. . . . Open my eyes to Your strength
and give me a new vision as I abide quietly in Your presence.*

Foolish Wisdom

Has not God made foolish the wisdom of the world?
1 CORINTHIANS 1:20 NIV

People have the wisdom of the world at their fingertips. Through the reach of the Internet, they can take classes at the world's best universities, listen to some of the most intelligent speakers, and read a large portion of all the best books ever written.

But having easy access to all of that hasn't seemed to make people all that much wiser. They still flounder in their foolishness and get caught up in their chaos. They're still, by and large, fighting against one another more than living in harmony. Somehow, everyone has all the answers, but no one can work out the solutions to the problems.

Why is that?

Well, it could be that they don't ask the one who is the source of all wisdom.

Just as in the days of the first disciples, people are still looking for signs. They look out in the world for answers, reasons, and evidence. They look to one another for guidance.

"But we preach Christ crucified" (1 Corinthians 1:23 NIV).

If you go to Jesus, you will find the answers. If you study His life, you will see the order to your chaos. If you accept His grace, you will find who you were meant to be: A seeming fool to the world. But, in reality, a wise woman of God.

God, if Your story is considered foolishness to
the world, then let me be a fool too. Amen.

God of Restoration

I will surely gather them from all the lands where I banish them in my. . .great wrath; I will bring them back. . . . They will be my people, and I will be their God. . . . I will make an everlasting covenant with them. . . . I will rejoice in doing them good and will assuredly plant them in this land with all my heart and soul.
JEREMIAH 32:37–38, 40–41 NIV

When we fall short of God's expectations, we experience feelings of shame and regret. Sometimes we get stuck in those feelings, because. . .surely, God is *still* mad at us. He will *never* forgive us. And, in the middle of our mess, we often feel like the worst humanity has to offer.

And yet, our God of judgment is also a God of restoration. He promises *both*—one is as sure as the other! As these verses from Jeremiah 32 remind us: Those who had been banished, He *will* gather them back together again. He *will* be their God; and they *will* belong to Him—along with future generations. He *will* bless them and do good to them. He *will* inspire them so they never turn away from Him. And He makes good on these promises!

If you're struggling today, take heart! Invite the God of restoration to draw you back to Him. He will—with all His heart and soul!

Father, thank You for always bringing me back to You.

Sweet Surrender

*Come to Me, all you who labor and are heavy-laden
and overburdened, and I will cause you to rest.
[I will ease and relieve and refresh your souls.]*
MATTHEW 11:28 AMPC

If you have ever stood under a powerful waterfall, the water—though it pummels your body—offers a sense of fresh renewal. Jesus said if you come to Him, He will refresh your soul. He offers spiritual rest. Unlike physical rest, one definition of *spiritual rest* is "to cease from striving."

Spiritual rest offers a place of sweet surrender. In his book *The Saints' Everlasting Rest*, seventeenth-century English Puritan church leader, poet, hymn writer, and theologian Richard Baxter said, "They who seek this rest [to cease from striving] have an inward principle of spiritual life. God does not move men like stones, but He endows them with life, not to enable them to move without him, but in subordination to himself, the first mover."

Jesus is calling you to a higher place of rest. As you move in Him and with Him, you can let go of those things you are trying to control and can experience His sweet, easy rest.

*Jesus, I want to experience the spiritual rest You have for
me. I let go of my control and submit to Your direction.
I stand under the waterfall of Your spiritual rest and
will not move except to do so in step with You.*

Unity with the Father

"Love your enemies and pray for those who persecute you,
that you may be children of your Father in heaven. . . .
Be perfect, therefore, as your heavenly Father is perfect."
MATTHEW 5:44–45, 48 NIV

The biggest challenge facing you today is probably a person—what she said or did, or didn't say or do—to you or someone you love. Relationships are difficult on any level—from someone you have never met who takes *your* parking place, to your closest friend who makes a disparaging remark about you, to your perfect prince who acts like a frog.

It's easy to get caught up in the drama when someone pushes your buttons or you feel used, abandoned, mistreated, or hurt. Society is full of people looking for revenge and a way to make someone pay for wrongs done to them. As a child of God, you can choose another way: your heavenly Father's way.

He responds with grace and forgiveness to both good and evil people. He is the calm in the middle of the storm. He desires to put His love, poured out lavishly upon you, to work *in* you and let it operate *through* you. You can rest in His peace, knowing He chose a perfect way for you.

Father, thank You for pouring Your love out on me.
I desire to walk in unity with You, allowing Your love
to flow through me and responding in peace to all.

Provisional Power

So Moses went out and told the people what the LORD had said. He brought together seventy of their elders and had them stand around the tent. Then the LORD came down in the cloud and spoke with him, and he took some of the power of the Spirit that was on him and put it on the seventy elders. When the Spirit rested on them, they prophesied—but did not do so again.

NUMBERS 11:24–25 NIV

Moses was feeling the weight on his shoulders pressing down upon him like a ton of bricks. The people he was trying to lead were complaining. The Israelites even started wailing over the fish they had gotten to eat in Egypt! The complaints of the people angered God and troubled Moses. So, he went before God, not knowing what to do. Then, God told Moses to tell the people to prepare for a miracle. The following day, the Israelites were given a provision of meat that lasted a whole month.

This miracle wasn't the result of anyone else's power, might, or strength. This amazing provision occurred through the power of God alone, giving you a glimpse of what the Holy Spirit can do.

Daughter, what do you find yourself grumbling about today? Go to God with all of your cares and concerns. He can handle them. Ask Him to turn your mundane messes into amazing miracle moments.

Abba Father, I need You! I need to witness more and more of Your provisional power in my life.

Right in Step with Your Guide

*The secret [of the sweet, satisfying companionship] of
the Lord have they who fear (revere and worship) Him,
and He will show them His covenant and reveal
to them its [deep, inner] meaning.*
PSALM 25:14 AMPC

In times of doubt, you may think your ship sailed without you, and you may be tempted to sink into a sea of regret. Instead, consider that perhaps it wasn't your ship that sailed after all.

How many times has someone literally missed a boat or plane and it saved his or her life? People missed the *Titanic* and lived to tell about it. What about those who didn't go in to work at the Twin Towers or missed their flight on one of the planes that crashed on 9/11?

When you find yourself in a place where you think you have "missed it," take a moment to look at it from a different perspective. You don't have to lose your peace over it. You can embrace the moment with a fresh perspective. With the Holy Spirit as your guide, you can rest in God's promise to reveal His purpose and plan. "In all things God works for the good of those who love him, who have been called according to his purpose" (Romans 8:28 NIV).

*Holy Spirit, lead me in the way I should go. I want to fulfill
my purpose. Thank You for revealing Your plans to me.*

Your Forever God

We pondered your love-in-action, God. . . . Your name, God,
evokes a train of Hallelujahs wherever it is spoken, near
and far; your arms are heaped with goodness-in-action. . . .
Our God forever, who guides us till the end of time.
PSALM 48:9–10, 14 MSG

When spending time in God's presence, you can feel His love and light reaching out and enfolding you. In response, you cannot help but praise Him for all He has done for you, in you, with you, and by you.

It seems almost impossible to imagine that God is with you now, surrounding you with His protection and strength. That He will be with you when it's time for you to cross over to heaven, giving you all the peace and comfort you need before being with Him in an entirely new way. And that He will be with you for all eternity, when there will be no more sorrow, pain, war, or death itself.

Although this constant presence of a living Lord may seem impossible, Jesus assures you that "all things are possible with God" (Mark 10:27 AMPC). So rest easy every moment of every day, knowing you will be forever guided by the one who loves you with all of His being.

Just thinking of Your constant presence, Lord, fills me with
such awe and comfort, peace and strength. I feel Your arms
surrounding me even now and am filled with eternal praise!

The Path before You

On the day the Tabernacle was set up, the cloud covered it.
But from evening until morning the cloud over the Tabernacle
looked like a pillar of fire. This was the regular pattern....
Whenever the cloud lifted from over the sacred tent, the people
of Israel would break camp and follow it. And wherever the
cloud settled, the people of Israel would set up camp.

NUMBERS 9:15–17 NLT

Back in the days of wilderness wanderings, God's presence resided in or hovered above the tabernacle. The Israelites followed the cloud when it rose above the tent, then stopped to rest when it settled back down.

Today, you can follow this pattern by staying near God both night and day. Although you may not have the tabernacle, you *do* have God's divine will, His Word, and His Spirit to direct and guide your soul in every area of your life.

Seek this path—the guidance of God's will, Word, and Spirit—and you will find your way through the wilderness as, at their command, you allow your heart to move or find its rest.

Lord, where You lead, I will follow. When You rest, I will rest.
Seeking Your will, focused on Your Word, and led by Your Spirit,
I no longer see the wilderness around me. Only Your path before me.

Nothing Is Wasted

At that time a great persecution arose against the church which was at Jerusalem; and they were all scattered throughout the regions of Judea and Samaria, except the apostles.

ACTS 8:1 NKJV

Dismayed that their neighbors had turned away from centuries of religious tradition, many in Jerusalem rose up to persecute Jesus' followers to the point that the Christians fled the city. While it was terrible at the time, in the end the Christians could echo Joseph's words, "You meant evil against me; but God meant it for good" (Genesis 50:20 NKJV). Because the Christians took the gospel wherever they went, their persecutors' attacks backfired spectacularly!

Jesus warned that Christians will experience suffering, especially persecution (see Matthew 5:10, John 16:33). But God's Word also promises that whatever happens, your story fits perfectly into the big picture of His plan (see John 9:1–3; Romans 8:28). Nothing is wasted, not your victories and hard work, your sins or pain or attacks from others. He fashions every part of your life for your good and His glory. Whatever you endure now, God will not waste it.

Will you open your pain to Your heavenly Father, trusting that He will use it beautifully as a conduit for His glory? Rest in and be empowered by His promise of working all things together "for good" (Romans 8:28), knowing that "He who promised is faithful" (Hebrews 10:23 NKJV).

Father, thank You for being the author of my story and that You are in charge of it all!

Work and Rest

Man goes out to his work and to his labor until the evening.
PSALM 104:23 NKJV

Way back in Genesis 2:3, God set a pattern for humans to follow: He worked six days and rested on the seventh. In Exodus, God commanded His people to "remember the Sabbath Day [the seventh day] by keeping it holy" (20:8 NIV) and to rest and worship on that day. In Ecclesiastes 3:1 (NIV) Solomon wrote, "There is *a time for everything*" (emphasis added).

God knows you need both work *and* rest (preferably, the daytime for work and the nighttime for rest, for doing so follows the natural rhythms of your body). For if you never work, your muscles will weaken; your mind, atrophy; your spirit, sadden. You will feel purposeless and empty. And yet, if you work all the time and never rest (ideally sleeping seven or eight hours each night *and* taking off at least one day per week), your body will fail you.

So go about your day and accomplish the tasks at hand. Whether you work in the home or outside of it, paid or unpaid, do all that lies before you today for the glory of God. But when it's time to rest, never feel guilty for doing so. God created man and woman. He made the day and the night. He created the first workweek, *and* the Sabbath was His idea!

God, help me find the right balance between work and rest. Amen.

This Is the Way

*The heart of the wise inclines to the right,
but the heart of the fool to the left.*
ECCLESIASTES 10:2 NIV

Perhaps you are tired of all the confusion life presents. Somehow, you may have lost your way, veered off the path. Distractions, selfishness, grief, and disappointment have pushed you in the wrong direction for too long. You lie in bed wide awake, unable to sleep, thoughts spinning around and around.

You turn off the droning television. Walk to the nearest prayer nook. Search for your Bible. Wait. It may have been a very long time since you have opened it. Perhaps the best place to start is with prayer.

You sit and have a chat with the one who has loved you since the beginning of time and longs to hear your voice. Tears flow. You begin to pray: "God, I'm lost. I'm confused. I'm sorry I stepped away from You. I need You. Please forgive me. Show me what to do."

Suddenly, you feel snug and warm in the once chilly house. You feel God's familiar embrace and hear a soft whisper: "I've always been with you." Your eyes open. Then you spy your Bible and, with a smile, pull it out from underneath a stack of books and begin reading.

*God, thank You for sticking with me all the way.
Help me keep my feet on Your path.*

God's Grace through the Detour

But he said to me, "My grace is sufficient for you,
for my power is made perfect in weakness." Therefore
I will boast all the more gladly about my weaknesses,
so that Christ's power may rest on me.
2 Corinthians 12:9 niv

You may be struggling. A situation is out of your control. Someone has made a decision that affects you—and you are not very happy about it.

Take heart. Such things happen often throughout life. You thought you were on a particular path, but the plans, circumstances, or parameters changed. And right now, you may feel as though God interrupted your life. But here's the thing: God always has permission to interrupt. And even though you may be having a hard time understanding what it all means, rest assured that you are just on a detour right now—and you cannot detour out of the reach of God's grace.

So there's no need to worry—a detour always puts you right back on the path you are supposed to be on! Your job is just to take this time to relax and enjoy the scenery.

God Almighty, when You interrupt my life with a detour, help
me to embrace it. I choose to trust You to take care of the details.
I let go of the expectations I have for this journey. Help me to
live in the moment and experience Your grace along the way.

Hope and a Future

"I will come to you and fulfill my good promise....
For I know the plans I have for you," declares the
Lord, "...plans to give you hope and a future."
JEREMIAH 29:10–11 NIV

Hope is beautiful. At times you see it, shining and bright, dancing ahead of you, making your steps lighter and forming a smile on your lips. These are the times when a new home, tiny new baby, or a new job fill you with expectation.

Other times, although hope may not seem apparent, it is still present. This is when you may be chilled deeply by grief, having lost a relationship, parent, or long-held dream. This is when the warmth of hope, like a well-worn quilt made by loving hands—God's hands—can be pulled around your shoulders, and you can rest under its comforting weight, snuggling up to the knowledge that one day you will again "see the goodness of the Lord in the land of the living" (Psalm 27:13 NIV).

God declares hope over, around, and through you. He has prepared a future for you and has plans for your well-being. A powerful as well as personal being, God doesn't give you someone else's future. He has made one just for you. Allow your heart to hope in Him and whatever future He has planned.

Father God, I thank and trust You for the future
You have planned for me. Please make my hope
a constant, in good times and bad. Amen.

Fully Equipped

*His divine power has given us everything we need for a
godly life through our knowledge of him who called us by
his own glory and goodness. Through these he has given us
his very great and precious promises, so that through them
you may participate in the divine nature, having escaped
the corruption in the world caused by evil desires.*

2 PETER 1:3–4 NIV

As Christians, we are fully equipped to live a godly life on earth. We don't have to live in a state of constant confusion. We don't have to stress about what to do or how to live. God has given us everything we need to be able to follow Him daily.

Second Corinthians 1:21–22 (NIV) tells us that "He anointed us, set his seal of ownership on us, and put his Spirit in our hearts as a deposit, guaranteeing what is to come." When we accept Christ as our Savior and Lord of our life, God gives us *His Spirit*! He places *His very own Spirit* in *our* hearts! Isn't that amazing? Take some time to fully reflect on that!

John 15:26 calls the Holy Spirit our "Helper." We are never alone. God's Spirit is right there with us as we make decisions, as we go about our day, as we face trials, and as we enjoy His blessings. We have a constant Helper everywhere we go!

*Heavenly Father, I'm amazed at what You've done.
Thank You for placing Your Spirit in my heart.
Help me to listen as You lead and guide me! Amen.*

The Worry-Free Life

Jesus said. . . , "Therefore I tell you, do not worry about your life, what you will eat; or about your body, what you will wear. For life is more than food, and the body more than clothes. Consider the ravens: They do not sow or reap, they have no storeroom or barn; yet God feeds them. . . . Who of you by worrying can add a single hour to your life? Since you cannot do this very little thing, why do you worry about the rest?
LUKE 12:22–26 NIV

What if someone else could handle the stresses and worries of your health, finances, relationships, work, politics—*all the things* that cause those pesky worry and frown lines to crease your forehead? No doubt you'd like to imagine what a worry-free life feels like.

Here's the beautiful thing: not only can you imagine it. . .you can actually *live* it! How? By giving every anxiety-inducing thought to Jesus.

The direction of your life will always mirror your strongest thoughts (see Proverbs 4:23)—and if those thoughts are worry-filled, you'll never be able to escape overwhelming fear and anxiety. When you create new pathways of thought, fully trusting the heavenly Father with your life, then this positive way of thinking will become your default. And the worry-free life will be yours for the taking!

Jesus, help me redirect my worried thoughts and fully trust You in the process. Thank You, Lord! Amen.

Thankful, Thankful Heart

I will praise you, Lord, with all my heart.
I will tell all the miracles you have done.
PSALM 9:1 NCV

If you live from the perspective that 10 percent of life is what happens to you and the rest is how you respond, then every situation has a side—positive or negative. Say you're late to work; every stoplight on your way is a red one; and you feel like you just can't make up the time. Instead of complaining, consider the delay was one that God appointed to keep you safe.

When you choose to approach life from the positive side, you can find thankfulness in most of life's circumstances. It completely changes your outlook, your attitude, and your countenance. God wants to bless you. When you are tempted to feel sorry for yourself or to blame others or God for difficulties, push PAUSE. Take a moment and rewind your life. Look back and count the blessings that God has given you. As you remind yourself of all He has done for you and in you, it will bring change to your attitude and give you hope in the situation you're facing. Count your blessings today.

Lord, I am thankful for my life and all You have done
for me. When life happens, help me to respond to it in a
healthy, positive way. Remind me to look to You and trust
You to carry me through life's challenges. Amen.

The Author of Time

*But do not forget this one thing, dear friends: With the Lord
a day is like a thousand years, and a thousand years are like
a day. The Lord is not slow in keeping his promise, as some
understand slowness. Instead he is patient with you, not wanting
anyone to perish, but everyone to come to repentance.*

2 PETER 3:8–9 NIV

These days everything is fast. Instant information is available at your
fingertips on the Internet. You have immediate communication with
friends through text messages. In this modern age, you are accustomed
to efficiency and quick answers.

But often, your deepest concerns and problems are resolved at what
seems to be a glacial pace. You pray and lay your needs before God. And
then, you wait for an answer. And wait. And wait some more. It may feel
like God is occupied elsewhere, putting out bigger fires. Eventually, you
might begin to think that God is indifferent to your daily struggles. But
this couldn't be further from the truth. Remember, God isn't bound by
time as you are.

His responses may seem painfully slow, but God is all-knowing and
He sees the span of eternity in infinite detail—whereas all you can see is
the moment before you. You can rest in the knowledge that His timing is
perfect, even if it may not feel that way.

*God, You are the author of time.
I place my life in Your capable hands.*

Call on God

*In the day of my trouble I will call
upon You, for You will answer me.*
PSALM 86:7 NKJV

Who do you call when you are in trouble? If your car breaks down, perhaps it's roadside assistance; but if your air conditioner breaks, it may be your HVAC company. What about when real trouble strikes? Do you hit speed dial and talk for an hour to your sister or best friend? Is it a parent you call or perhaps a mentor from church? None of these are bad phone calls to make in times of need—as long as you remember that first and foremost, you are to take your troubles to God.

God is there for you night and day. His Word tells you He never sleeps. When you are depressed or lonely, He's there. When you don't know what to do, He's there. There's no trouble you could encounter that would cause God to turn His back on you. He's ready and waiting for you, His daughter, to call out to Him.

Think about the best earthly father you know. Would that daddy desert his children in a time of need? Would he ever be too busy to come running? How much more does your heavenly Father long to attend to the needs of His own?

*God, I know that You are always ready to help. May You
be the first one I turn to with my troubles. Amen.*

Heart Work

Be alert and on your guard; stand firm in your faith (your conviction respecting man's relationship to God and divine things, keeping the trust and holy fervor born of faith and a part of it). Act like men and be courageous; grow in strength!
1 CORINTHIANS 16:13 AMPC

You have found God, you love living in His light, and you are firm in your faith. But you see people you love making choices that don't seem aligned with God's Word. And nothing you say seems to have any effect. How do you cope? What do you do?

You could lose a lot of sleep with worry. Or you could try another tack and go to God, praying: "Lord, it's so hard to watch someone I love choose things she knows are wrong. Why does it seem her heart is so hard toward you? Yet, I know that she belongs to You and that You love her more than I do. So I leave it in Your hands. Help me to trust You."

Deep down in your heart, you listen for the Lord's promising reply: "I'm taking care of it. No worries." Then you open your eyes, confident in His promise, and let Him do the heart work.

Lord, help me not to overthink things. It's not my place to make things happen in the lives of those I love. Only You can work in the heart. Thank You for peace to trust Your plan.

Plans for Good

"Don't you see, you planned evil against me but God used those same plans for my good, as you see all around you right now—life for many people."
GENESIS 50:20 MSG

Joseph made a powerful statement in today's scripture reading. It takes great maturity to see his life through spiritual eyes, able to see God's plan through his messy life. It reveals his complete surrender to God's will above his own desires. And it's a great example for us today.

Think about tough situations you've walked through. Maybe you're in one right now. Take inventory of the spine-weakening and spirit-breaking situations and how they've challenged your peace and joy. Are those what you focus on the most? Do they determine your mood and attitude? Are you angry? Are you trying to control and manipulate these circumstances to your favor?

If you responded like Joseph, you'd choose to trust that God allowed these trials only for your benefit and His glory. You would choose to believe He is always in the driver's seat. You'd adopt a position of surrender and activate your faith in God's will and ways. And at the end of the day, no matter how messy it was, you'd embrace the truth that He will use everything planned for evil. . .for good.

God has you, sister. He sees you. He loves you. And He's protective of His girl.

Lord, please give me spiritual eyes to see
Your good over the world's evil every time.

Awestruck with Wonder

*The whole earth is filled with awe at
your wonders; where morning dawns,
where evening fades, you call forth songs of joy.*
PSALM 65:8 NIV

We serve a remarkable God! His mighty hand is at work in creation around us. With the tip of a finger, He draws canyons out of rock. With just a breath, He moves ocean waves to and from the shore. With just a word, He bids the sun and moon to light our path.

The evidence of God's trustfulness is clear if we're paying attention. The tide continues to roll in, day after day. The sun continues to rise, morning after morning. Dew covers the earth in a cool, damp blanket, causing things to grow. Trees shoot up in magnificent splendor, shedding their leaves in autumn and springing back to life after snowy winter frosts melt away.

All of nature stands as a testimony to the fact that God is trustworthy, from the tiny caterpillars to majestic mountain peaks. If He can take care of even the smallest creature, if He can remind the moon to cast its glow, surely He can care for you even when you walk through dark valleys.

*Lord, I'm awestruck when I think about Your creation!
Ocean waves crash in joyous praise. Shimmering rays of
sunlight cast their beams across waving fields of wheat.
All of creation sings in grateful chorus, Father, and I'm
overwhelmed by it all. What a mighty God You are! Amen.*

Cities of Refuge

The following cities were designated as cities of refuge:
Kedesh of Galilee, in the hill country of Naphtali;
Shechem, in the hill country of Ephraim; and Kiriath-
arba (that is, Hebron), in the hill country of Judah.
JOSHUA 20:7 NLT

No doubt everything felt foreign to the Israelites when they crossed over into the Promised Land. At any point, something could go wrong. (They must have been frightened and hesitant because of all the unknown variables.) So, God designated refuge (sanctuary) cities, places of safety, healing, and recuperation. The Israelites could always run to these safe places to rest and catch their breath.

God is still in the "cities of refuge" business. When things happen that are out of your control, He provides a safety net, a place you can run to. Jesus is your safe place. He's your city of refuge, your shelter from the storm. When you're in trouble, run to Him. When you're feeling lost, race to His arms for guidance. When you're broken, confused, and unsteady on your feet, let Him be that city of refuge to undergird you.

And while you're at it, keep proclaiming the message that God is a sanctuary for all. Let love lead the way as you guide others to Him so that they too can find rest.

Thank You for being my city of refuge, Lord.
I'm so grateful to have a place to run. Amen.

Strengthened by the Lord

*Because God helped the Levites, strengthening them as they
carried the Chest of the Covenant of God, they paused to
worship by sacrificing seven bulls and seven rams.*

1 CHRONICLES 15:26 MSG

The ark of the covenant was not too heavy for the men carrying it. So why does the Bible tell us that God *helped* them carry it? In what ways did they need strengthening?

These same men had witnessed Uzzah fall dead for merely touching the ark to steady it (see 1 Chronicles 13:9–10)! The remaining Levites probably trembled at the thought of transporting it. But God calmed their fears. He *strengthened* them emotionally and mentally for the task. Not only this, but He *helped* them.

Often, when you are going about the business of the church, you may forget God. Although you are capable of carrying out a lot of well-laid plans in your own human strength, let this verse serve as a reminder for you to seek and rely on God's help.

You may not feel you need God to assist you. But without God, you wouldn't take your next breath, much less carry out the missions you may have created in your own limited thinking. So before you stumble, reach out to the Lord. Ask Him to lead, guide, and strengthen you on the way.

*Heavenly Father, help me in all I do today. You are my strength,
my steady rock, my ultimate helper. In Jesus' name I pray, amen.*

Wise Ways

"Leave your simple ways and you will live;
walk in the way of insight."

PROVERBS 9:6 NIV

Wisdom, as quoted in Proverbs 9:6, invites you to turn from the confusion of a hectic lifestyle to walk a different path. She compels you to live the life of abundance that you are designed for. You are invited into her home where she has set a banquet feast specially prepared for you. She asks you to dine with her, to "leave your simple ways."

The "simple ways" from which Wisdom wants you to detour are a life lived without insight, thought, or understanding. Such a life is like a house with its windows shuttered, doors boarded up, and furniture covered. When the shutters are thrown aside, doors opened, and furnishings exposed by Wisdom, light, air, and color flood throughout the house. Dark corners are illuminated. Purposes become clearer. Priorities are set in order. Confusion is replaced with meaning.

So explore God's truths through His Word. Pause throughout your day to think about Him. Walk with Wisdom and she will help you to understand. In so doing, you will discover your great worth in God, comprehend life's meaning and richness, and realize that God has a plan for you to know Him and abide in Him. These truths will bring peace of mind and insight to everyday problems.

God, give me wisdom to leave any simple
ways and open my life to You. Amen.

High Expectations

"They found grace out in the desert. . . . Israel,
out looking for a place to rest, met God out looking
for them!" GOD told them, "I've never quit loving you
and never will. Expect love, love, and more love!"

JEREMIAH 31:2–3 MSG

Grace out in the desert. What a refreshing thought. Have you been in a desert place, lost, lonely, disappointed, feeling the pain of rejection? Often, our immediate response is to berate ourselves, look within to see how we have been the one lacking, plummeting our self-esteem. Dejected, we crawl to that desert place to lick our wounds.

Behold! God is in our desert place. He longs to fill our dry hearts with His healing love and mercy. Yet, it's so hard for us—with our finite minds—to grasp that the Creator of the universe cares for us and loves us with an everlasting love, no matter what.

Despite their transgressions, God told the Israelites He never quit loving them. That is true for you today. Look beyond any circumstances and you will discover God looking at you, His eyes filled with love. Scripture promises an overwhelming, unexpected river of love that will pour out when we trust the Lord our God. Rest today in His word. Expect God's love, love, and more love to fill that empty place in your life.

Father, we read these words and choose this
day to believe in Your unfailing love. Amen.

Set Free

*"I removed the burden from their shoulders;
their hands were set free from the basket."*
PSALM 81:6 NIV

God reached down and saved the Israelite people from slavery in Egypt. He led them out of the land when the time was right. The Exodus began with Him, through Moses, instructing the people in some strange ways. Following His directions, they smeared the blood of a Passover lamb around their door frames. They prepared unleavened bread. They walked right up to the edge of a raging sea and passed through on dry land. They looked back over their shoulders to see their pursuers swallowed up by that same great body of water.

Your God is a burden remover. He does not desire for you to remain enslaved to addiction or abuse. He wants to part the waters before you and provide safe passage. He may calm the storm and beckon you to walk on the water, or He may hold you close and calm you in spite of the storm that causes destruction all around you.

If you are downcast, look up today! Find God there, ready to call you His child, ready to loose the chains of that which binds you. Find Him faithful. Release your burden to the one who has the power to cast it out of your life.

*Burden-removing Father, free me from that which
plagues me today. In Jesus' name I pray, amen.*

Constant and Continual

Jesus, replying, said to them, Have faith in God [constantly].
MARK 11:22 AMPC

This faith thing isn't a once-and-done deal, nor is it something to be thrown away at the first sign of trouble or forgotten when all is well. It's a persistent, dogged, determined belief in God.

This faith is the constant belief that a beneficent force, one that sustains and propels everything around you—from the tiniest of ant colonies to the farthest of planets—is blessing, guarding, watching, and keeping you; smiling down, bursting to favor you with gifts galore; looking you in the face and giving "you peace (tranquility of heart and life *continually*)" (Numbers 6:26 AMPC, emphasis added).

Your only part is to be constant in your faith. And the only way to do that is to spend lots of time with God. When you do, His part is to be continually giving you peace—within and without—no matter what is going on in your life.

God has created you to be with Him, so abide in Him. He has given you His Son, Jesus, to guide you in all things, so follow Him. He has left behind His Spirit to comfort you, so cling to Him. This faith is fed and fueled by you actively spending time with the greatest of beings—Father, Son, and Spirit. Do your part (He is already doing His) and you will have a constant, living faith and a continual, abiding peace.

Here I am, God. Let's talk.

Promises Fulfilled

*Not one of all the LORD's good promises to
Israel failed; every one was fulfilled.*
JOSHUA 21:45 NIV

When was the last time you broke a promise? If you are like most people, it does happen from time to time, and undoubtedly more often than you would like.

Sometimes, it's very hard to keep promises. Circumstances interfere. People, places, times, and availability change. You can't control all the factors, and so that promise you made suddenly slips out of your hands.

But God's promises are not like yours. He does not make promises that He cannot keep. And He keeps every promise that comes from His lips.

Do you know what promises God has made to you? Read His Word. Search for the promises of love and compassion, forgiveness and grace, reward and suffering. For He does not just promise good things will come. He also tells you that you will have trouble. You will be tempted. You will suffer for His name. But like the Israelites who had struggled for so long and spent so much time fighting their way into the Promised Land, you will also find rest on every side. If you stay with Him, He will rescue you and bring you to a land of peace. It's a promise.

*God, I want to remember Your promises.
Help me, too, to keep my word. Amen.*

An Unseen Pathway

Your road led through the sea, your pathway through the mighty waters—a pathway no one knew was there!
PSALM 77:19 NLT

You have read the story. The Israelites, fleeing bondage in Egypt, arrive at the edge of the Red Sea with the Egyptians on their heels. At just the right moment, God parts the sea and every last Israelite passes through to the other side! And in the next instant, their pursuers are caught up in the raging waters, horses and chariots along with them.

Great story. Nice tale of long ago. Awesome movie clip. But wait. This is more than a fantasy. It really happened! And the miraculous part is that God still makes paths for you today.

When you find yourself between a rock and a hard place, cry out to God. When circumstances lead you to a dead end, lift your eyes toward heaven. God is the "great I AM," meaning that He is what you need in each moment. In times of anxiety or fear, you need the Prince of Peace. Other times, when filled with gratitude, you sing praises to the King of Glory.

Then there are Red Sea moments. At such crossroads, rely on Yahweh, the Lord who provides unseen pathways and makes a way where there seems to be no way (see Isaiah 43:16–20)!

God, remind me that You are truly a God of miracles. In my Red Sea moments, I trust You to make a way. Amen.

The Best Plans

When your days are over and you go to be with your ancestors,
I will raise up your offspring to succeed you, one of your own
sons, and I will establish his kingdom. He is the one who will
build a house for me, and I will establish his throne forever.
1 Chronicles 17:11–12 niv

David wanted to build a temple to house the ark of the covenant. He felt guilty that he was living in a fine home built of cedar and that the ark had no home. His heart was in the right place. But God had other plans.

The prophet Nathan delivered God's word to King David that his son Solomon was the one God would allow to build the temple. God wanted a man of peace to construct it. Although the message wasn't exactly what David expected, it pleased him nonetheless. The warrior David accepted Nathan's news and was beyond thankful to the Lord for establishing his family to be used in God's service.

Even if you feel your plans are God-centered and for His glory, He may have His reasons for thwarting them. So if something isn't going the way you had envisioned, resist the urge to blame God. Trust Him. He will use you as He sees fit. His choices and His timing are always perfect.

God, help me rely on Your wisdom rather than
my own, for You see the big picture. Amen.

God's Partner

In everything we do, we show that we are true ministers of God.
2 CORINTHIANS 6:4 NLT

When you turn on the television to glimpse the evening news, you are immediately reminded of the fallen world you live in. Danger, calamity, and terror are all around, yet you have hope in God's mercy because you know who you are.

- You are God's partner (see 2 Corinthians 6:1).
- You patiently endure troubles, hardships, and calamities of all sorts and sizes (see v. 4)
- You know that God's power is working in you (see v. 7).
- Your heart may ache, but you have eternal joy (see v. 10).
- You may be poor but give spiritual riches to others (see v. 10).
- You may own little but have everything (see v. 10).
- You have no lack of love within you, even though others withhold their love from you (see v. 12).

In other words, as God's partner, you see the world with His eyes. You know He's living in you. He's your safety zone. As you abide in Him, nothing can touch you.

So, as God's partner, don't panic. Instead, praise Him for what He is doing in your life. And continue to show others that no matter what happens in the world, you have peace because you are a true woman of the Way.

Father, thank You for allowing me to be Your partner in patience, power, joy, richness, and love as I abide in You.

I Am Your God

Fear not [there is nothing to fear], for I am with you; do not look around you in terror and be dismayed, for I am your God. I will strengthen and harden you to difficulties, yes, I will help you; yes, I will hold you up and retain you with My [victorious] right hand of rightness and justice.
ISAIAH 41:10 AMPC

Have you ever woken up in the middle of the night and found yourself unable to get back to sleep? The previous day's conversations, events, what-ifs, and more are playing over in your mind, keeping Mr. Sandman at bay.

That's when you know the challenge is on. You get up quietly, careful not to disturb your snoring dog, cat, husband, child—whatever—and head for where you left your Bible the night before. You sit down and open God's Book to the verse above, then read Isaiah 41:13: "For I the Lord your God hold your right hand; I am the Lord, Who says to you, Fear not; I will help you!" (AMPC). Having set a firm foundation of faith, you enter into the Psalms, reading aloud King David's words of praise. As the minutes tick by, you feel God's presence. As you abide in Him, your eyes grow heavy and you find sleep in His arms.

Father, sometimes I live in my head. I let my worrisome thoughts take over. Thank You for bringing me back into Your presence, strength, and peace.

Divine Faithfulness

*A calm and undisturbed mind and heart are the
life and health of the body. . . . Wisdom rests [silently]
in the mind and heart of him who has understanding.*
PROVERBS 14:30, 33 AMPC

As Timothy's mentor, it was important for Paul to be up-front about the dangers of the last days. In 2 Timothy 3, we read Paul's perspective about what those days might look like: people will love only money and themselves, as well as be disobedient, mockers of God, cruel, prideful, and more. Paul goes on to give to Timothy a charge that expresses Paul's faith and trust in God: "You must remain faithful to the things you have been taught. You know they are true. . . . You have been taught the holy Scriptures from childhood, and they have given you the wisdom to receive the salvation that comes by trusting in Christ Jesus" (2 Timothy 3:14–15 NLT).

In today's Old Testament reading, we learn that through it all, there's hope for God's people for their Redeemer is strong (see Jeremiah 50:34). No matter what you might be walking through today, as you trust God, the Holy Spirit will give you calmness and an undisturbed mind and you'll receive the benefits of silent wisdom and understanding.

*Lord, when I trust You, I receive divine peace. Please give
me the strength and faith to continue to trust You and
Your Word, no matter what's happening in my life.*

Be the Voice of Reason

And when he came near her, the woman said, Are you
Joab? He answered, I am. Then she said to him, Hear the
words of your handmaid. He answered, I am listening.
2 SAMUEL 20:17 AMPC

At David's command, Joab was tracking down Sheba, a troublemaker who'd rebelled against the king. They tracked him to the town of Abel of Beth-maacah, where he was hiding. As the Israeli forces began tearing down the city wall, a wise woman spoke up as a voice of reason. She reminded Joab the city was peaceful, and she offered to deliver the fugitive in a different way. Later that day, Sheba's head was thrown over the wall.

Had the wise woman of Abel not spoken up, chances are the historic city would have been left in shambles. It was her courage to come forward and the perspective she shared that preserved the wall from further damage. This lone woman had the wherewithal to set emotions aside and speak with wisdom.

It's not always easy to take a step back from a situation to get a thirty-thousand-foot view. But when we do, it allows us to see the big picture. We're removed from the chaos of high emotions and able to see things more clearly. And it's in that clarity we can bring logic and truth to the discussion.

Lord, I want to be the voice of reason within my circle of influence.
Help me take a breath so I can offer sound advice and good sense.

Shining Brightly

The light of the righteous shines brightly,
but the lamp of the wicked is snuffed out.
PROVERBS 13:9 NIV

Great beauty is seen in the flame of a candle, the glow of a firefly, or a twinkling star. You are a light that shines brighter than these because of the righteousness of Christ. Steady and sure, your flame glows with the glory of Christ in you.

Your unquenchable light is made for eternity. This world will not satisfy your eternal soul. Focus on what is lasting—God's love, His Word, and the spirits of His people. Take time for each in your day. When you focus your effort on what is lasting, you carry it with you into eternity.

Make time to hear your child's discovery. Hold the hand of an elderly neighbor. Seek out a quiet moment and listen to the secrets of someone's heart—maybe even your own. Ask God to reveal Himself in His Word. These moments will make your heart happy.

You are transformed by trials, your rich golden light deepening with endurance. You are stronger than you think and more vivid than you can imagine. Never be intimidated by the darkness around you. It's no match for you. You were made to shine forever, so don't hide your glory.

Father God, thank You for making me to live eternally with You.
Help me to focus on the things that last forever. Amen.

In Control

And while they were there, the time came for her to give birth. And she gave birth to her firstborn son.
LUKE 2:6–7 ESV

Joseph took Mary, his betrothed wife, to Bethlehem for political reasons. He didn't really have much choice in the matter; if he'd failed to register them, he'd have broken the law. But even though it looks like politics ruled their circumstances, we know better. God orchestrated everything—including the time and place required for the census—in order to fulfill His plan.

Sometimes it may feel like we're controlled by our jobs, our schedules, or somebody's political agenda. But God is in control! He knows what He's doing, and we can trust that He's working all things together for our good and His glory.

Just as the prophets foretold Christ's birth in Bethlehem, God already knows every step of our lives. He knows tomorrow and next week and next month and next year, and He is lining things up to do something great in our lives. Like Mary and Joseph, all we need to do is follow Him, do our best each day, and trust His plan. Just as He brought everything together on that night, He is pulling all things together to fulfill His purpose in our lives.

Dear Father, thank You for having a plan for my life. Remind me that You're in charge, even when it feels like other things are controlling my life. Help me to trust You and follow You. Amen.

The Gift of Sleep

In peace I will lie down and sleep.
PSALM 4:8 NLT

God infuses variety into our body clocks just like He does with other aspects of our personhood. So for every night owl, there is somewhere a morning lark or a hummingbird (those in the middle). And that way, all the jobs on earth get done and there is always someone awake with the needed energy and creativity. It would really be sad if no one could take the midnight shift at the hospital or if no one could get up at four in the morning to milk the cows!

Still, no matter the rhythm of one's internal clock, all of us need sleep. Our bodies require sleep to renew themselves and recharge for the next day. According to the National Sleep Foundation, while we are sleeping, tissue growth and repair occurs, energy is restored, hormones are released, appetite is balanced, and the immune system gets a charge. It is normal to spend about one-third of our lives sleeping.

And when you think about it, God did plan the nighttime for our benefit, right? In the beginning, He separated the darkness and light and gave each a place in the cycle of a twenty-four-hour day. And though He never needs to rest, we do. We cannot do the 24-7 thing; we weren't meant to. And as long as God sustains the earth, there will always be tomorrow in which to work.

*Lord, let me praise You by getting the proper rest
for my body so that I may be at my optimum level of
energy and creativity for Your glory. Amen.*

God Is Good

Praise the Lord, for the Lord is good;
sing praises to His name, for it is pleasant.
PSALM 135:3 NKJV

We hear it in church. We say it to others. We want to believe it. God is good. All the time.

The Bible says it, so we know it is true. Jesus lived it so we could see it in living color. But sometimes, when life yanks hard and pulls the rug out from under us, we begin to doubt. And that is probably a normal human temptation. Though we know that good parents discipline their children and sometimes allow them to learn "the hard way," we expect God, our heavenly Father, to do it differently.

So we need reminders. And He put them in our world everywhere we turn, at unexpected junctions and in the most ordinary places. Warm sunshine, brilliant flowers, rainbows after storms, newborn babies, friendships, families, food, air to breathe, pets, church dinners, sunrises, sunsets, beaches, forests, prairies, mountains, the moon and stars at night and puffy clouds in the day. All around us are hints that God is good and that His works are beautiful and life-giving.

When disease or tragedy or hardship enters our lives, we can rest assured that God is not the author of these destructive things and that someday, He will cleanse this globe of its misery and set everything right. Until then, He has given us His strength, His hope, and His promise. That is enough to keep us going.

Father God, I praise You. You are good. Your works are
wonderful. I know You love me. Help me to trust Your
plan and purpose for me. In Jesus' name, amen.

Relax

"You will not have to fight this battle. Take up your positions; stand firm and see the deliverance the Lord will give you."
2 CHRONICLES 20:17 NIV

Why do we always feel we need to fight our own battles?

Oh, God wants us to use common sense and stand up for others and ourselves when it's appropriate. But sometimes, it's best not to defend ourselves at all. Sometimes, when we know we've done no wrong, when we know we stand innocent before God in whatever situation we find ourselves, it's good just to remain still and calm and let God be our defender.

Truly, the more we defend ourselves, the guiltier we sound sometimes. But when we can stand before God with clean hands and a pure heart, God will deliver us. Oh, it may not be in the way we want. It may not happen as quickly as we'd like. But when we decide to stand firm, to continue living godly lives, to continue seeking His approval in our words, thoughts, and actions, we can trust Him.

Let's remember today to rest in His goodness, despite the battles that rage around us. We don't have to live our lives fighting. We can relax. Our Father is the judge, and He will deliver us.

Dear Father, thank You for being my defender.
Thank You for delivering me from all sorts of trouble.
Help me to relax and let You take care of me. Amen.

Waiting for Hope

When life is heavy and hard to take, go off by yourself.
Enter the silence. Bow in prayer. Don't ask questions:
Wait for hope to appear. Don't run from trouble. Take
it full-face. The "worst" is never the worst.
LAMENTATIONS 3:28–30 MSG

Jeremiah wrote today's verses when he was mourning the fall of Jerusalem. The prophecies he had preached for years had come to pass, and his heart was broken. We'd all be wise to listen to his response.

When disaster strikes, do you go into fight-or-flight mode? Perhaps you respond somewhere in between.

Jeremiah suggests *both* responses. When life is "heavy and hard," he lists six steps to prepare you to "take it, full-face."

To get ready to fight, you must first retreat. That means to (1) go off by yourself, (2) get quiet, (3) pray, (4) be still, and (5) listen for God's voice. Allow His promises to sink in. And (6) wait for hope to fill your tank.

Only after your retreat are you equipped to face the problem. You won't run from it, ask questions, or try to make sense of it. You just take it head-on—and realize the worst is never the worst. It can't be. God is by your side.

Heavenly Father, right now life seems heavy and hard.
Let me retreat into You and wait for Your hope to appear
so that I will be ready to face what lies ahead.

Your Time with God Shows

*When Moses came down from Mount Sinai carrying the two
Tablets of The Testimony, he didn't know that the skin of his
face glowed because he had been speaking with G*OD.
EXODUS 34:29 MSG

Moses' face literally glowed from his time with God. He was visibly marked from that experience, enough so that others could literally see it. What a powerful visual it must have been for the Israelites to look on his face and understand the profound effects spending time with the Father had.

Your face may not sparkle and shimmer after being with God; but make no mistake, your life does reflect it. It will make you a more loving wife and patient mom. You'll be a more faithful friend and trustworthy confidant. It will give you wisdom to share with others and courage to do the hard things. Investing your time with the Lord will help you become kinder, willing to extend grace and forgive others faster.

How could this investment benefit your life and relationships? What would need to change in your schedule to allow for it? And what would happen if you decided not to make room for time with God?

If your goal is to be more like Jesus and point others to Him, then be sure to make spending time with the Lord a priority.

*Lord, I am sorry for not giving You the time You deserve.
Forgive my mixed-up priorities. I am committed to spending
time with You every day because I want my life to reflect it.*

Serenity

"They will be like a tree planted by the water that sends out its roots by the stream. It does not fear when heat comes; its leaves are always green. It has no worries in a year of drought and never fails to bear fruit."
JEREMIAH 17:8 NIV

Jeremiah paints a beautiful picture with his words. He describes what life is like for those whose trust is in the Lord, those who have full confidence in Him. This idyllic scene brings comfort and hope to the reader. It is a message of peace and serenity. A tree planted by water will never thirst; it will never fear excessive heat because it remains hydrated. No matter what, it will always bear fruit and thrive.

You will be like that tree if you trust in the Lord fully, knowing He will always care for you and meet your needs. Thus, you need not stress.

Psalm 1:3 (NIV) contains similar words to those of Jeremiah 17:8, saying that they who delight and meditate on God's law are "like a tree planted by streams of water, which yields its fruit in season and whose leaf does not wither—whatever they do prospers."

Fully trust in God, live in His Word, and then revel in His peace. Ah. . .that's better.

Dear Lord, take me to that place of peace where I trust in You with full confidence. With You, I have no reason to fear.

God Sees It All

"And He said, 'Look up and see: all the males that are mating with the flocks are streaked, spotted, and speckled, for I have seen all that Laban has been doing to you.'"

GENESIS 31:12 HCSB

How refreshing to know God sees everything others have done and are doing to you. You may be suffering in silence—afraid to tell others—but nothing misses God's eye. That means He sees the mean-spiritedness and gossip. He sees the rejection and abandonment. God sees it when people try to lead you astray or lie to your face. He sees the betrayal you're walking through as well as the hurtful words spoken to you.

He is a safe place to hide. God is your tower and refuge, a place where you can be protected. He always cares about and for you, and He is the one who will give you the courage and confidence needed to take the next right step.

Think about who or what is challenging you today. Where are you suffering alone? Who is taking advantage of you? Where are you feeling overwhelmed? Trust that God sees every second of these moments and that He's ready, willing, and able to help.

Lord, it's so comforting to know You're always with me. Sometimes, I forget and try to endure the hard moments and seasons all by myself. Would You remind me that You see everything and that You love me enough to engage when I need You?

Few Things Are Needed

"Martha, Martha," the Lord answered, "you are worried and upset about many things, but few things are needed—or indeed only one. Mary has chosen what is better, and it will not be taken away from her."
LUKE 10:41–42 NIV

When you think of the word *many*, what comes to mind? Many joys? Many sorrows? Many challenges? Many faith-moments?

Our lives are filled with "many" things to do. We're overwhelmed with tasks. And in this crazy fast-paced world, we work double-time to keep up with those around us. We want to prove our worth through our busyness.

In this story of Mary and Martha, we get God's perspective on busyness. "Mary has chosen what is better." Those words ring out as a reminder that God cares more about the "few" things that are needed. In fact, He boiled it down to one critical thing: spending time in His presence.

The next time you're tempted to do the "many" things (and at a rapid pace, no less) pause a moment and think about these two sisters. Has God called you to be a Martha. . .or a Mary?

Lord, I admit I often focus on the "many" things that need to be done and not on the "few" that are truly necessary. Spending time at Your feet is far more important than racing through each day exhausted and frazzled. Shift my focus, Father, as I let go of the things robbing me of my time with You. Amen.

Go Ahead, Take a Break

*Six days you shall do your work, but the seventh
day you shall rest and keep Sabbath, that your ox
and your donkey may rest, and the son of your
bondwoman, and the alien, may be refreshed.*
EXODUS 23:12 AMPC

Life moves at ninety miles an hour. Our calendars are maxed out with everything from sports practices to work schedules to doctor visits to volunteer hours. Too often, we have to be in four places at the same time, and the pace is killing us. No wonder we're exhausted, overwhelmed, and cranky.

God created Sabbath with great intentionality. He knew we must have much-needed downtime on a regular basis to stay at our best. Even God—when creating the heavens and earth—took a break. The truth is we are not God. We simply don't have endless energy and focus. We need to be deliberate to schedule our own Sabbath because God will use it to restore us.

You may curl up and read a good book or take a hike to enjoy nature. You might sleep and make it a pajama day. You might even rock on the porch, listen to your favorite music, or get a massage. There may be every excuse to not do it, but what if you did? And how might God bless you through it?

*Lord, thank You for knowing how important it is to
take a break. It's hard to make that kind of time for
me, so I'll need Your help to make it happen.*

Take a Look

Bless the Lord, O my soul! O Lord my God, you are very great!
You are clothed with splendor and majesty, covering yourself with
light as with a garment, stretching out the heavens like a tent.
PSALM 104:1–2 ESV

When the psalmists felt overwhelmed and needed to be reminded of God's greatness, they looked around them—past the busyness of life, past the day-to-day toils and troubles, past the evil that abounded. . .past all of that—to the ways God was revealed in His creation.

Psalm 104 gives a panoramic view of how God created and cares for earth and everything on it. His many acts include forming the solid ground, shaping the mountains and valleys and seas with a command, making gushing springs and plentiful vegetation, and ordering the days and seasons. Yes, God's fingerprints are everywhere! So much so that the psalmist declared, "O Lord, how manifold are your works!"; "O Lord my God, you are very great!" (v. 24; v. 1).

What do you do when you're overwhelmed? Do you head to the spa? Do you hunker down with a good book or a gooey brownie? Do you hit the gym or maybe some high notes while singing in the shower? For a change, do what the psalmists did. Step outside. Look around at God's creation. And let your heart praise Him.

God, I see Your greatness in the sky, in the ocean. . .
in this whole world. How awesome You are! Amen.

Daughter of the King

"For the LORD your God is living among you. He is a mighty savior. He will take delight in you with gladness. With his love, he will calm all your fears. He will rejoice over you with joyful songs."

ZEPHANIAH 3:17 NLT

Look at all the promises packed into this one verse of scripture! God is with you. He is your mighty Savior. He delights in you with gladness. He calms your fears with His love. He rejoices over you with joyful songs. Wow! What a bundle of hope is found here for the believer. Like a mother attuned to her newborn baby's cries, so is your heavenly Father's heart for you. He delights in being your Father. He knows when the storms of life are raging all around you. He senses your need to be held close and for your fears to be calmed. It is in those times that He is for you a Prince of Peace, a Comforter. He rejoices over you with joyful songs. Can you imagine that God loves you so much that you cause Him to sing? God sings over you. And the songs He sings are joyful. He loves you with an unconditional, everlasting love. Face this day knowing that your God is with you. He calms you. And He sings over you. You are blessed to be a daughter of the King.

Father, thank You for loving me the way You do. You are all I need. Amen.

Crossing Over

But you will cross the Jordan and settle in the land the Lord your God is giving you as an inheritance, and he will give you rest from all your enemies around you so that you will live in safety.

DEUTERONOMY 12:10 NIV

God promised the Israelites a land filled with milk and honey, a place they could call their own. He led them through the wilderness and pointed them toward their ultimate destination. When they reached the Jordan River, however, the Israelites hesitated.

How many times have we done the same? God brings us through wilderness experiences and points us toward a place filled with promise, but we hesitate, overcome with fear. We can see the fulfillment of promises ahead. We know our future is filled with possibilities. But we stand frozen in place, unable to move.

The same God who led you through the desert can be trusted to carry you to the next phase of your journey. He's got amazing things in store for you. Say goodbye to fear. Take hold of His hand, and cross the Jordan to an amazing new adventure.

Father, I'll admit it: There have been many "Jordans" in my life that I refused to cross. I got to the very edge and lost my nerve. I was afraid to step over the invisible line. Thank You for giving me the courage to cross over into new and exciting seasons in my life, Lord. From now on, I choose to trust You! Amen.

Solution to Life's Problems

What can I say for you? With what can I compare you, Daughter Jerusalem? To what can I liken you, that I may comfort you, Virgin Daughter Zion? Your wound is as deep as the sea. Who can heal you?
LAMENTATIONS 2:13 NIV

Everyone experiences tough times, days when things seem bleak and there appears to be no way to escape despair. In those times, many may seek to commiserate with friends or family and take some solace in the fact that others are worse off. While this is small consolation, it *is* consolation nonetheless. Yet, as well-meaning as those friends or family members are, their advice does not solve your problems.

The accounts related in the book of Lamentations make it clear the people of Jerusalem were going through tough times. However, their struggle would not last forever. God alone was the solution to their problems. God alone was able to heal their afflictions.

God alone can help you too. Allow Him to uplift you right now with these words: "I will restore you to health and heal your wounds" (Jeremiah 30:17 NIV).

Dear Lord, sometimes I feel overwhelmed by hardship and can see no way out. Please open my eyes to see You and my ears to hear You. I trust that You will heal me and restore peace in my life. I have faith, Lord, that no matter how bad things look, I truly am blessed and am grateful for Your presence in my life.

Talking to the Father

The prayer of a righteous person is powerful and effective.
JAMES 5:16 NIV

We have all had those inevitable days when we are exhausted or discouraged and it seems too hard to carry on. We might feel as dry as the desert sand, with nothing left to give. This is a time when we could use nourishment for our souls.

The prophet Zechariah said, "Ask the Lord for rain in the springtime, and he will answer with lightning and showers." Matthew Henry explained this scripture: "Spiritual blessings had been promised. . . . We must in our prayers ask for mercies in their proper time. The Lord would make bright clouds and give showers of rain. . .when we seek the influences of the Holy Spirit in faith and by prayer, through which the blessing held forth in the promises are obtained."

When these times hit, use "knee mail." Don't just "tweet" a short sigh to the Lord, but carve out some time to pray, to praise, and to petition our heavenly Father for strength to carry on. He is faithful to answer our pleas and send refreshment to our hearts. It could be in the form of a restful night's sleep, a friend or relative to exhort and encourage, or a stranger's greeting. We never know how the Lord will answer our petitions, but answer He will. God's inbox is never too full.

Dear Lord, how we long for Your presence. Father, hear our prayers this day; extend Your hand of mercy to me. Amen.

He Cares for You

You yourselves have seen what I did to Egypt,
and how I carried you on eagles' wings
and brought you to myself.
EXODUS 19:4 NIV

Often, we feel deserted. As though God doesn't hear our prayers. And we wait. When Moses led the children of Israel out of Egypt toward the Promised Land, he did not take them on the shortest route. God directed him to go the distant way lest the people turn back quickly when things became difficult. God led them by day with a pillar of cloud and by night with a pillar of fire. How clearly He showed Himself to His children! The people placed their hope in an almighty God and followed His lead. When they thirsted, God gave water. When they hungered, He sent manna. No need was unmet.

The amount of food and water needed for the group was unimaginable. But each day, Moses depended on God. He believed God would care for them.

If God can do this for so many, you can rest assured that He will care for you. He knows your needs before you even ask. Place your hope and trust in Him. He is able. He's proven Himself over and over. Read the scriptures and pray to the one who loves you. His care is infinite. . .and He will never disappoint you.

Heavenly Father, I know You love me and
hear me. I bless Your holy name. Amen.

Turn toward God

Therefore say thou unto them, Thus saith the Lord
of hosts; Turn ye unto me, saith the Lord of hosts,
and I will turn unto you, saith the Lord of hosts.
ZECHARIAH 1:3 KJV

The word *repentance* means to turn away from that which has been hindering a right relationship with God, asking for forgiveness and turning back to Him. It is, in essence, looking up instead of looking down. It's freedom instead of bondage. As one turns back to God and His ways, God might seem closer and more real than ever before. Yet, His grace can be overwhelming at times.

Those living during Old Testament times had to adhere to many religious rituals. They had to go through a long, tedious process to experience peace, cleanliness, and good standing with God.

For you, dear sister in Christ, yesterday might have been like any other day. Or perhaps it wasn't. Maybe you almost lost your temper, thought about saying or doing something that would go against what you knew was right. What was the end result? Did you lose your cool or not? If you did, guess what? There's an opportunity to turn back to God. All you need to do is call Him.

Father, I look up to You to fill my mind, mouth, and heart
with Your goodness. When I make a mistake, help me
be humble and turn to You for forgiveness. Then show
me how to make things right. . .in Your sight.

Slow Down

She is clothed with strength and dignity;
she can laugh at the days to come.
PROVERBS 31:25 NIV

As women, we often find ourselves weighed down by concerns regarding our families, careers, friendships, and other aspects of our lives. We worry about illness, whether our kids will have friends in school, and if we should change jobs. We try to make sure we're saving the right amount of money and planning correctly for the future.

There's nothing wrong with planning and preparing. But God would have us clothed with strength and dignity and able to laugh at the future. If that's the complete opposite of your current existence, it's time to slow down, grab a coffee, and spend more time in the Word of God.

God doesn't want you to live in a constant state of panic about the future. He tells us in Matthew 6:34: "Therefore do not worry about tomorrow, for tomorrow will worry about itself. Each day has enough trouble of its own" (NIV).

So breathe in deep and exhale all those worries away. Clear your head and heart. God's got you! Plan and prepare. But cast your worries on His shoulders. Be so completely confident in Him that you can laugh at the days to come!

Lord, help me to lay my concerns at Your feet.
To put all my days in Your hands. I pray You
would replace my worry with laughter. Amen.

Respite

The Lord said to Moses, "Speak to the Israelites and say to them: 'These are my appointed festivals, the appointed festivals of the Lord, which you are to proclaim as sacred assemblies. There are six days when you may work, but the seventh day is a day of sabbath rest, a day of sacred assembly. You are not to do any work; wherever you live, it is a sabbath to the Lord.' "

LEVITICUS 23:1–3 NIV

Through Moses, the Lord gave His people a solid foundation on which they can live a balanced life. This structure permits you six days in which to work but declares that on the seventh day, you should rest for your well-being. It is a respite from everyday life and gives you a chance to slow things down from earthly activity.

In this fast-paced world, it is important to take some time for yourself and to give thanks to God for His many blessings. How wonderful that you can hit PAUSE on the remote control of your life and enjoy some quiet time with Him. Through God's grace, you have the foundation for a well-lived, balanced life. Empowered through God's perfect structure, you can be the best you can be.

Dear Lord, help me structure my life based on your unshakable foundation created just for me. Thank You for considering my every need, both spiritual and physical, and for this day of rest. Amen.

The Perfect Redeemer

*"Who are you?" he asked. "I am your servant Ruth,"
she replied. "Spread the corner of your covering
over me, for you are my family redeemer."*
RUTH 3:9 NLT

Ruth was a woman of faith. After suffering the loss of her husband, she could have wallowed in grief and misery. Instead, she chose to follow her mother-in-law, Naomi, to a place where she knew no one, in order to honor her late husband (and, perhaps, the God he had introduced her to).

Ruth was also a woman of action. She worked hard to glean in the fields, toiling with intention and consistency. The owner of the fields, Boaz, noticed her work ethic and was impressed. Later, Ruth followed Naomi's advice and found Boaz at night while he was sleeping. Because he was a relative of hers and a man of integrity, he agreed to spread his covering over her as her "family redeemer." This meant he promised to marry and take care of Ruth (and Naomi).

Ruth's story has much to teach us. Just as Ruth moved on from grief to action, we can ask for God's help to move past our own losses and not get stuck in bitterness or anger. With His help, we can honor others and not wallow in self-pity or destructive habits. Also, as His strength and forgiveness cover our weaknesses and failures, we can find peace and joy. He is the perfect Redeemer who takes care of us so we don't have to worry about providing for ourselves.

*My rock and Redeemer, I praise and thank You for
Your covering over me. You are a faithful provider.*

Pray for His Return

The end of all things is near. Therefore be alert
and of sober mind so that you may pray.
1 PETER 4:7 NIV

World peace is an ever-present concern and likely one that God's people take to Him in prayer. It seems overwhelming to pray for something that appears impossible, but when Christians pray for peace, they pray knowing that Jesus will fulfill His promise of coming back. How long will it take for Him to return? No human knows. In the meantime, Christians persistently pray for His return and try to live peacefully in a chaotic world.

Around 600 BC, Jerusalem fell to the Babylonians. The Jews were exiled to Babylonia and held captive for seventy years. God told the prophet Jeremiah to tell His people to settle there and live normally. He said they should seek peace in the place in which they lived until He came back to get them (Jeremiah 29:4–7).

Today's Christians are similar to those Jews. They live normally in an evil world seeking peace on earth while holding on to the promise of Jesus' return.

Paul wrote, "Brothers and sisters, whatever is true, whatever is noble, whatever is right, whatever is pure, whatever is lovely, whatever is admirable. . .think about such things. . . . And the God of peace will be with you" (Philippians 4:8–9 NIV).

May God's peace be with you today and every day until Jesus comes.

Lord, may Your kingdom come and the
earth be filled with Your glory. Amen.

Unfailing Love

Let your unfailing love surround us,
Lord, for our hope is in you alone.
PSALM 33:22 NLT

We hope that our sports team will win the big game and that Starbucks will bring back its hazelnut macchiato. We also hope that our jobs will continue to fulfill us and pay our bills and that God will answer a heartfelt prayer with a long-awaited yes. Whatever we're hoping for, it's easy to think that God doesn't care about the details of our lives. However, just as a parent cares about everything that happens to her child, so God longs to share every part of our day. Why not talk to Him about all our needs and desires?

As we sip our morning coffee, we can jot down thanks for morning blessings such as flavored creamers and hot water for our shower. While we do our jobs, we can regularly bring our concerns (and co-workers) before God's throne. We could keep scriptures scribbled on sticky notes in our cubicle—or on our desk—to remind us to think with God's thoughts throughout the day instead of falling back on worldly patterns. When we lay our head on the pillow at night, we can voice the answered prayers which grace our lives, drifting off to sleep, grateful for God's unfailing love.

Those small, simple actions add up to a day filled with hope and gratitude. . .and those days add up to a life well-lived.

Father God, thank You for Your unfailing love. Thinking on
that love, which I haven't earned and can't repay, causes
me to fall to my knees in hope, gratitude, and joy.

A Thankful Mind

Let the peace of Christ rule in your hearts, since as members
of one body you were called to peace. And be thankful.
COLOSSIANS 3:15 NIV

How do we let the peace of Christ rule in our hearts? One way is to take every thought captive and make it obedient to Christ (see 2 Corinthians 10:5). That means when an unkind or impure thought comes into our minds, we take it straight to the cross of Christ.

Instead of obsessing over conversations and what other people might be thinking of you, you focus on Jesus. Sometimes, just saying the name of Jesus out loud when you have a negative thought can stop the thought in its tracks and refocus your mind.

After allowing Jesus into your thought process, thank God for your blessings. Thank Him for His great love for you and others. Ask Him to give you something else to think about instead of going back to that original thought.

If you're having a convicting thought, take that to God as well. Ask Him to reveal what is true and right and what your response should be.

Surrendering our thoughts to Christ naturally leads to surrendering our actions to Him too. When our hearts and minds are surrendered to Christ, the peace of Christ is free to rule in our lives.

Thank You, God, for meeting me in each moment. Let my heart
be set on You. Allow my heart and mind to be full of thankfulness
for who You are and all that You've done in my life. Amen.

Whiter Than Snow

Take away my sin, and I will be clean.
Wash me, and I will be whiter than snow.
PSALM 51:7 NCV

If you've ever looked out over a pristine, white field covered in glistening mounds of white snow, you know what purity looks like. Everything underneath those mounds of snow has disappeared from view, to be seen no more. The white snow covers it all, making it irrelevant.

That's how forgiveness works. When we come to God and confess our sins, He is faithful and just to forgive us. His forgiveness washes over us in exactly the same way that the snow covers the ground below. All traces of yesterday—the awful things we've done, the pain we've caused, the heartache we've gone through—are gone. In place of the bad memories is glistening white forgiveness, sparkling with the hope of better days to come.

If you haven't yet asked Jesus to be the Lord of your life, if you haven't accepted His forgiveness for the sins you've committed, this is the perfect day—the perfect season—to do so. He can wash your sins away and leave you whiter than snow.

Father, I love the image of snow that I find in this scripture. It's a reminder that my past really can be in the past. I want to live for today, Lord, so that I can have the courage to step into tomorrow without worrying about what happened yesterday. Cleanse me, Lord!

I Grow Weary

*But those who wait for the Lord [who expect, look for,
and hope in Him] shall change and renew their strength
and power; they shall lift their wings and mount up [close
to God] as eagles [mount up to the sun]; they shall run and
not be weary, they shall walk and not faint or become tired.*

ISAIAH 40:31 AMPC

Jesus said come to Him and He would give us rest. Being in His presence, trusting in Him, brings us the rest He desires for us. We can only find this rest when our spirits are in tune with His Word.

As long as we are warring inside, we will not find rest. We must find out what Jesus wants for our lives and then obey. Feasting on His Word and learning more about Him will give us the direction we need and the ability to trust. It is only when we understand our salvation and surrender that we can come to Him, unencumbered by guilt or fear, and lay our head on His chest. Safe within His embrace, we can rest.

Each new day, He will give us the strength we need to fight our battles just as His presence will refresh our spirits. We will be as a well-watered garden, refreshed and blessed by our loving Creator.

*Father, I am weary and need Your refreshing
Spirit to guide me. I trust in You. Amen.*

Nothing Better

I know that there is nothing better for people than to be happy and to do good while they live. That each of them may eat and drink, and find satisfaction in all their toil—this is the gift of God.
ECCLESIASTES 3:12–13 NIV

Did you wake up this morning with a light heart? Adam and Eve woke every morning with a joyful heart until sin entered their garden paradise. You, however, have troubles, struggles, and problems to solve each day. Your life has unanswered questions, obstacles, and hardships. With all that going on, how can you enjoy the day He's made (see Psalm 118:24)?

Rely on God to take care of you. Choose to lift your face to your heavenly Father and trust Him. Tell Him aloud that you're thankful for His provision.

Put a new spin on your work and its meaning by considering it as God's gift to you. What do you enjoy about what you do? Thank God for what's been placed in your hands, and your joyful mood will flourish.

To find even more satisfaction and joy, look for opportunities to bring more good into your day. "Good" can be as simple as connecting with a friend, sharing a smile with a child, or thanking God for a simple meal. Be intentional about enjoying today!

God, help me be open to new ways of thinking about today's work. Help me develop a joyful heart and attitude every moment of my life.

Unexpected Plans

This is how the birth of Jesus the Messiah came about: His mother Mary was pledged to be married to Joseph, but before they came together, she was found to be pregnant through the Holy Spirit.
MATTHEW 1:18 NIV

What an exciting time for Mary and Joseph. Planning a wedding, dreaming of their future home, future children, future joys. Mary may have tucked things away in a hope chest; Joseph probably worked and saved and prepared to support his future bride. And then. . .oh my.

Sometimes, God's plans for us are unexpected. Even when it seems we're going along, following the right path, doing everything as best we can according to God's policies, all of a sudden, *bam*! Something hits out of left field.

God's plans for us don't always make sense in the moment. We feel overwhelmed. We may even feel betrayed by God. But in moments like these, we must fall back on our faith. We draw on the experiences we've had, which show us that He loves us, and that He is always good. We pull from the stories of those who've come before us, who have lived through similar crises, and who have seen from beginning to end that God's love never changes, never fails.

If Mary and Joseph's plans hadn't been interrupted by this unexpected event, they wouldn't have gotten to parent the Son of God. Next time some unforeseen calamity strikes, take a deep breath and a deeper dose of faith. Then, sit back and wait for the blessing.

Dear Father, help me to trust You even when circumstances surprise me. Amen.

Trusting in Trials

Blessed is the one who perseveres under trial because, having stood the test, that person will receive the crown of life that the Lord has promised to those who love him.

JAMES 1:12 NIV

Often, we as believers walk through seasons that are trying and cumbersome. James' words above extend grace and encouragement to us to live out our faith— even under pressure-filled situations. Because it's in those moments that faith is tried, tested, and refined.

Have you ever found it challenging to trust God during a trial? Chances are you have. Can you recall how you got through the test? Chances are you have a testimony that was cultivated, that came bubbling over from those pressure-cooker situations. In fact, chances are that one of the key ingredients that got you through was trusting God.

If you're walking through a trial right now, trust God. Even if you don't feel it, speak it. Consider saying these words out loud: "Lord Jesus, even though I don't feel it, I'm choosing to trust You. Even though my heart is heavy and my soul is weak, I surrender all."

Lord, may the words of my mouth and the meditations of my heart be pleasing to You. By faith, I thank You for blessing me with trials, believing such tests will be used to help me trust You more. I look forward to the testimony You have in store.

Speak, Wait, Hear

Eli said to Samuel, "Go, lie down; and it shall be, if He calls you, that you must say, 'Speak, L<small>ORD</small>, for Your servant hears.' " So Samuel went and lay down in his place.
<small>1 S</small>AMUEL<small> 3:9</small> NKJV

In the Old Testament, God dwelled in the temple and spoke to specific people at specific times. But in the New Testament, the Word took on flesh. It began to live among God's people. It took the form of a human being called Jesus. John wrote, "And the Word (Christ) became flesh (human, incarnate) and tabernacled (fixed His tent of flesh, lived awhile) among us; and we [actually] saw His glory (His honor, His majesty)" (1:14 AMPC).

Gone are the days when we have to travel to a church, temple, or tabernacle to speak to the one who was, is, and always will be. For having accepted Christ, God now dwells within us, leading us, guiding us, hearing us. But are we listening?

You may know who God is, but have you ever heard Him speak into your life? If you have, you know how amazingly wonderful that can be. Ask God to speak through His Word. Let Him know you're listening. Trust that He is within you, around you, beside you. Speak, and then wait quietly and patiently until you get a response, until you see the light He is so longing to give.

Speak to me, Lord. I'm waiting to hear Your sweet voice.

Get above It All

*Set your minds and keep them set on what is above (the
higher things), not on the things that are on the earth.*
COLOSSIANS 3:2 AMPC

If you've ever taken a trip by airplane, you know with one glimpse from the window at thirty thousand feet how the world seems small. With your feet on the ground, you may feel small in a big world; and it's easy for the challenges of life and the circumstances from day to day to press in on you. But looking down from above the clouds, things can become clear as you have the opportunity to get above it all.

Sometimes, the most difficult challenges you face play out in your head—where a struggle to control the outcome and work out the details of life can consume you. Once removed—far away from the details—you can see things from a higher perspective. Close your eyes and push out the thoughts that try to grab you and keep you tied to the things of the world.

Reach out to God and let your spirit soar. Give your concerns to Him and let Him work out the details. Rest in Him and He'll carry you above it all, every step of the way.

*God, You are far above any detail of life that concerns me. Help me
to trust You today for answers to those things that seem to bring me
down. I purposefully set my heart and mind on You today. Amen.*

Scripture Index

OLD TESTAMENT

NEW TESTAMENT